Training the 21st
century police
officer.

Training the 21st Century
Police Officer

Redefining Police Professionalism for the Los Angeles Police Department

Russell W. Glenn

Barbara R. Panitch

Dionne Barnes-Proby

Elizabeth Williams

John Christian

Matthew W. Lewis

Scott Gerwehr

David W. Brannan

Prepared for the
City of Los Angeles and the
Los Angeles Police Department

Public Safety and Justice
RAND

This report was prepared for the City of Los Angeles and the Los Angeles Police Department by RAND Public Safety and Justice, 1700 Main Street, P.O. Box 2138, Santa Monica, CA 90407-2138.

RAND is a nonprofit institution that helps improve policy and decisionmaking through research and analysis. RAND® is a registered trademark. RAND's publications do not necessarily reflect the opinions or policies of its research sponsors.

Published 2003 by RAND

Cover design by Peter Soriano

ISBN: 0-8330-3468-5

On June 15, 2001, the City of Los Angeles signed a consent decree with the United States Department of Justice. The consent decree is essentially a settlement agreement that aims to promote police integrity and prevent conduct that deprives persons of rights, privileges, or immunities secured or protected by the Constitution or laws of the United States. Areas for remediation are identified and expeditious implementation of corrective measures is required. This project is the result of the mandate of one paragraph in the decree that requires an independent examination of police training in the areas of use of force, search and seizure, arrest procedures, community policing, and diversity awareness. RAND conducted this study over a nine-month period (July 1, 2002–March 31, 2003).

This study will be of interest to Los Angeles City residents and those in the Los Angeles City government. It also has national application for the field of police training.

This project was funded by the City of Los Angeles on behalf of the Los Angeles Police Department.

RAND PUBLIC SAFETY AND JUSTICE

This study was conducted within RAND's Public Safety and Justice unit. RAND Public Safety and Justice conducts research and analysis that helps inform policymakers and communities in the areas of public safety, including law enforcement, terrorism preparedness, immigration, emergency response and management, and natural disasters; criminal justice, including sentencing and corrections policy, firearms, and community violence; and drug policy, which focuses on problems related to illegal drugs and substance abuse. Inquiries regarding RAND Public Safety and Justice may be directed to

Jack Riley
RAND Public Safety and Justice
1700 Main Street
Santa Monica, CA 90407-2138
310-393-0411
www.rand.org/psj

CONTENTS

Appendix

FIGURES

TABLES

This book summarizes a nine-month study conducted by RAND for the Los Angeles Police Department (LAPD, also hereafter referred to as the Department). The City of Los Angeles entered into a consent decree with the U.S. Department of Justice. The objective of this book is to provide analyses and recommendations to assist the LAPD in meeting the requirements outlined in paragraph 133 of this decree, ultimately enabling the LAPD to better serve the interests of the people of Los Angeles through improved training in five critical areas. These areas are use of force, search and seizure, arrest procedures, community policing, and diversity awareness.

Early in our investigation, it became apparent that many of the Department's training problems share a common foundation. Even though the problems encompass many varied topics and training challenges, they are systemic in nature and require a unified approach to change. We recommend that the LAPD clearly and consistently communicate expectations for appropriate LAPD officer behavior. Many officers conduct themselves in a manner that community and Department norms would deem appropriate. Others do not. We suggest that the first essential step to improving police training is to establish and communicate a common foundation for police performance—a redefined professionalism.

Police professionalism as described herein refers to a very specific and widely recognized construct. It is distinct from the notion of police professionalism that was prevalent in 1950s and 1960s policing. The police professionalism that we posit instead is Samuel Huntington's (1957) far wider ranging three-tiered approach based on the tenets of corporateness, responsibility, and expertise.

Not everyone accepts that police can attain professional status. However, many, the authors among them, find evidence to support a more positive perspective. Los Angeles Chief of Police William J. Bratton concurs, plainly stating that he "resents the concept that policing is not a profession."[1]

The Huntington concept of professionalism provides the basis for communicating the meaning of service as a police officer in the City of Los Angeles. Other organizational and leadership philosophies fit within this concept to include ethics-based, integrity-centric community policing. Competency-based training is also related to these endeavors. Professionalism accepts that personnel cannot be trained for every event, but they must be prepared to handle any eventuality, to think on their feet, and to react with appropriate legal, moral, and ethical behavior. The authors realize that advancing a notion of a redefined professionalism may unsettle some who see the old professional era of policing as a failed model. Nevertheless, we trust that most will understand that what is presented herein is a much needed new start and potentially very effective means of molding a force that will serve the people of Los Angeles well.

The governing concept of this new professionalism will provide an important underpinning for correction of weaknesses within the LAPD training realm. One overarching and five primary recommendations form the basis for addressing these shortcomings. Each is complemented by numerous additional and more detailed supporting recommendations. Appendix M provides a consolidated listing of all such recommendations for ease of reference.

The following is our overarching recommendation:

> The Los Angeles Police Department should adopt a concept of police professionalism that incorporates the tenets of corporateness, responsibility, and expertise as the mechanism for guiding the development and execution of its training, to include training

---

[1]William Bratton, interview with Barbara R. Panitch and Russell W. Glenn, Los Angeles, Calif., February 13, 2003.

in the areas of use of force, search and seizure, arrest, community policing, and diversity awareness.

The five primary recommendations are

- Establish an LAPD lessons-learned program.

- Introduce and maintain consistently high quality throughout every aspect of LAPD training.

- Restructure the LAPD Training Group to allow the centralization of planning; instructor qualification, evaluation, and learning retention; and more efficient use of resources.

- Integrate elements of community-oriented policing (also called "community policing") and diversity awareness training models throughout LAPD training.

- Develop training on use of force, search and seizure, and arrest procedures that meets current standards of excellence.

This study employed a combination of data collection methods including a review of LAPD and other departments' written course documents, Department policies, and protocols; observation of instructional sessions; focus groups with police department personnel; interviews with police managers, elected officials, and community members; a case study survey of best practices in the field of policing, both domestic and international; and literature reviews in the areas of adult and police education, policing, use of force, search and seizure, arrest, community policing, and diversity.

Though the five primary areas of study were listed as separate entities in the consent decree, they are in practice not discrete areas of training any more than they are discriminate parts of service on the streets. The five subject areas constitute a core set of competencies that an ethical and effective police officer will regularly employ in concert. We address them accordingly within this book. The days of mandating a given number of hours on community policing, use of force, or other topic areas of concern are past. Such artificial "stovepiping," where naturally intertwined topics are handled separately, runs counter to common sense, policing reality, and effective service to society as the client. The new police professionalism requires a greater training sophistication just as it demands greater sophistication of understanding from city government personnel overseeing law enforcement activities, police leaders, and officers on the street.

Conducting training founded on police professionalism is of value only if LAPD's senior leadership stands behind and champions the concept. Department leaders with whom the authors came in contact during the conduct of this study unhesitatingly demonstrated willingness in this regard. There is much reason to believe that a department already proficient in many ways can improve yet further with such leaders at the top and training that promotes the pursuit of professionalism throughout the force.

ACKNOWLEDGMENTS

Timely completion of this study would not have been possible without the dedication and hard work contributed by many individuals. Los Angeles Police Department Training Group personnel, including Sergeant Gena Brooks, Director Robin Greene, Caryn McLeod, Captain Sergio Diaz, and Assistant Chief George Gascón, assisted greatly throughout the process. Many other members of the Department contributed through their participation in interviews, focus groups, and by graciously allowing classroom or other training observation.

Edmund Edelman, William Geller, Dennis Nowicki, Robert Stewart, and Elizabeth Watson served as a sounding board for findings and, drawing on their many years in police and civil government positions, acted as valuable guides to police culture. Estela Lopez provided excellent insights and entrée for community issues in the relevant areas. Ellen Scrivner and Dina Levy served as peer reviewers for the final report. We thank them for their aid in the quality assurance process.

RAND staff critical to the production of this book and other project efforts include Clifford Grammich, Terri Perkins, Christina Pitcher, Louis Ramirez, and Meg Matthius. These individuals have enhanced our work considerably. A special thanks to Deirdre B. Glenn for her assistance in helping to proofread portions of the study.

Finally, we wish to thank those members of the City of Los Angeles team who assisted by providing selfless oversight of this project and all, from the City of Los Angeles and elsewhere, who kindly participated in interviews, project meetings, or otherwise assisted in this undertaking for the people of Los Angeles and their police department. A special thanks to Mayor James K. Hahn, Chief William J. Bratton, and Los Angeles City Council Member Cindy Miscikowski for taking the time to contribute.

ARCON	Arrest and control
CALL	Center for Army Lessons Learned
CAPRA	Client, acquiring and analyzing, partnerships, response, assessment
CED	Continuing education division
CEDP	Continuing Education Delivery Plan
CP	Community-oriented policing
C-PABs	Community-Police Advisory Boards
FTO	Field training officer
IDC	Instructor-development course
LACP	Los Angeles Community Policing
LAPD	Los Angeles Police Department
LD	Learning domain
LETAC	Law Enforcement Tactical Application Course
LMS	Learning management system
OIC	Officer in charge
PACCTs	Police and community collaborative teams
POST	Peace Officer Standards and Training
PTO	Police Training Officer

RCMP	Royal Canadian Mounted Police
RFP	Request for proposal
ROI	Return on investment
SARA	Scanning, analysis, response, assessment
SLO	Senior lead officer
SOAR	Staff Officers' Annual Retreat
WPLP	West Point leadership program

Chapter One

BACKGROUND AND METHODOLOGY

> Together we will build on the legacy and the traditions and the skills
> . . . . We will take that most famous shield, the most famous badge
> in the world—and whatever little . . . tarnish exists, it will be wiped
> clean, and it will be the most brilliantly shining badge of any in the
> United States.
>
> > William J. Bratton,
> > upon his appointment to position of Chief of
> > Police of the Los Angeles Police Department,
> > October 28, 2002

Half a century ago, the Los Angeles Police Department (LAPD, or "the Department") and its version of professionalism were models for police agencies worldwide. Law enforcement and the concept of police professionalism have since changed. So, too, via several significant events, has the reputation of the LAPD.

The change in the standing of the Department was confirmed by the *United States of America v. City of Los Angeles, California, Board of Police Commissioners of the City of Los Angeles, and the Los Angeles Police Department Consent Decree of June 15, 2001* (the "consent decree"). This wide-ranging document mandates the implementation of many changes across the LAPD. Paragraph 133 of that document, that portion of concern to this study, requires that

> Within 18 months of the effective date of this Agreement the Department shall audit police officer and supervisory officer training, using independent consultants who have substantial experience in

1

the area of police training. The audit shall assess: ways in which LAPD training could be improved (i) to reduce incidents of excessive use of force, false arrests, and illegal searches and seizures and (ii) by making greater use of community-oriented policing training models that take into account factors including paragraph 117(c).

The factors cited in paragraph 117(c) are

cultural diversity, which shall include training on interactions with persons of different races, ethnicities, religious groups, sexual orientations, persons of the opposite sex, and persons with disabilities, and also community policing.[1]

Succinctly, the mandate is to scrutinize Department police training in five areas: use of force, search and seizure, arrest, community policing, and diversity.

Numerous commissions and work groups have examined LAPD training over the last decade.[2] Some of the better known include the work of the Christopher Commission and the Rampart Independent Review Board. These many sources have provided several hundred recommendations pertinent to LAPD training. Many are unique. Some are contradictory. Others are repetitive. Still others are no longer needed or valid.

Our book is therefore merely the latest of numerous evaluations of Department training, all of which have similarly sought to improve the education provided to Los Angeles police. Many of our observations are very similar to those raised previously by the Christopher, Rampart, and other undertakings.[3] It is likely that any further efforts will yield similar results until identified shortcomings are remedied.

We took two deliberate steps in an effort to make our contribution as valuable and pertinent as possible. First, we deliberately chose not to review in-depth the conclusions of other studies until after developing our own findings and recommendations. Second, because

---

[1]The consent decree, 2001, pp. 55, 61.

[2]Robin Greene, Director of Police Training, LAPD, interview by Barbara R. Panitch, February 10, 2003.

[3]These are mentioned in several cases identified in the pages that follow.

many LAPD problems are systemic in nature and require solutions at a fundamental level, we identify the most common shortfalls, explain their character, and provide a single unifying concept that the LAPD should incorporate in addressing them. That theme is professionalism. This concept provides a way of taking many seemingly separate issues and linking them in a logically comprehensible whole.

SETTING THE CONTEXT

The training problems facing the LAPD are not entirely unique. National case studies indicate that other law enforcement agencies regularly wrestle with the same or similar issues. It is also important to acknowledge the concerted and genuine efforts of many members of the LAPD, city government, and citizens of Los Angeles to improve their police agency. Many have the will to improve. It is necessary to identify and pursue the best way to do so.

Los Angeles benefits from a heterogeneous and dynamic character that adds vibrancy to its economic and cultural life. It also explains why the city confronts many issues previously seen only internationally and why Los Angeles experiences many law enforcement challenges before the rest of the country does. The unique character of the city gives the LAPD the opportunity, and responsibility, to be a leader in policing and to develop ethical, legal, and innovative responses to these emerging needs. It also puts it in a position to establish examples for other major domestic and international departments. As a world class city, Los Angeles can also benefit by learning lessons from others. Fifty years ago, many people thought that the LAPD could solve all of its problems from within. Today the Department must understand that it has as much to learn from outside as it has to offer. Our findings and recommendations draw on innovations and lessons learned elsewhere, both from inside and outside the law enforcement community.

THE FOUNDATION'S CORNERSTONE: A COHERENT APPROACH TO IMPROVEMENT

The Los Angeles Police Department Training Group labors under a myriad of proposals and recommendations, now including those that will follow here. It is critical that an organizing principle and leadership vision guide implementation in order to introduce co-herency and consistency in training messages. We found this orga-nizing principle heretofore lacking. Initial classroom observations indicated an absence of a unifying theme for officer development. Focus group sessions with probationers, field training officers, and other personnel corroborated this finding. Finally, individual inter-views pointed to a struggle in developing a consistent leadership vi-sion for Department officers (partly, and understandably, due to administration changes). That the LAPD does not successfully com-municate a unified message creates a dangerous vacuum that indi-vidual officers fill with their own interpretations of proper behavior. While the consent decree itself acknowledges that the great majority of officers conduct themselves in a manner that community and De-partment norms would deem appropriate, some officers do not. The consent decree recognizes the need for the LAPD to better instill in-tegrity throughout the department. A clearly, consistently articulated unifying professional ethic will help considerably in meeting these aims. Chapter Two provides an overview of modern police profes-sionalism. This concept has three fundamental tenets. Chapters Three, Four, and Five provide analyses of the tenets' application to LAPD training in the areas of use of force, search and seizure, arrest procedures, community policing, and diversity awareness.

Chapter Two: Law Enforcement Professionalism and the LAPD

The concept of police professionalism evolved throughout the twen-tieth century. In its earlier years, policing was based on a "political model" in which officers were assigned to neighborhoods and grew intimately familiar with their "beats." Decisions about police ser-vices for a community were made by political bosses.[4] Policing during this period was characterized by overwhelming political in-fluence and, too often, corruption.

The subsequent so-called "professional" era of policing was a direct response to this political control and manipulation of city law en-forcement agencies. Reforms included outfitting police officers in

---

[4]Seattle Police Department, 1996.

readily identifiable uniforms. Departments took advantage of the increased availability of cars and assigned more officers to vehicle patrol, in part because they were thereby easier to supervise. Standards of conduct were instituted, including the International Association of Chiefs of Police Law Enforcement Code of Ethics that was considered one of the greatest accomplishments of that era.[5] The code specified a standard for ethical and legal police conduct. Paramilitary command and control structures became prevalent. Officers were educated to do as they were told and not question authority.

Police analyst George Kelling believes it is more appropriate to characterize this period as one of "reform" rather than professional policing.[6] It created many new problems even as it addressed many of those from the political era. Critics claim that the reform model created professionally remote, internally oriented, legalistic, formalized, and rigid police departments in the efforts to prove integrity and efficiency. The Los Angeles Police Department became the epitome of this "professional" model, its officers emblematic of the police experts who demanded "just the facts."

The civil unrest of the late 1960s accented these shortcomings in the reform model. Police in the political era had often been too involved with community politics. Now they were frequently too removed from the society they were to serve. Departments did not reflect the racial mix of the communities they served. Police might have been technically proficient but they too often lacked requisite communications skills. Officers often had problems communicating effectively with the diverse elements of American society.[7]

Efforts at reform gradually shifted to community policing approaches. The basic strategy was one of partnership with those served and included goals of identifying and solving problems mutually recognized as important.

It is the spirit of August Vollmer's professionalism (see Kelling and Coles, 1996, p. 75) that underlies this shift and the concept of profes-

---

[5]Ibid.

[6]Kelling and Coles, 1996, p. 75.

[7]Fyfe et al., 1997, p. 16. This dichotomy of competence continues to affect policing today.

sionalism as it is presented in the pages that follow. His tenets of serving a higher purpose, rigorous education for officers, broad police discretion, and collegial control are similar to the universal concept of professionalism described by Samuel Huntington and recognized in many vocations.

Chapter Three: Corporateness

Corporateness is the first considered of the three components that define professionalism. Corporateness involves instilling an understanding of professional duty and building a minimum level of expertise in an individual before he is admitted to the profession. It thereafter demands collectively maintaining established standards of performance. Implementation of the concepts underlying corporateness takes many forms. In Chapter Three, we focus on three critical aspects of training necessary to instilling and maintaining a sense of corporateness: (1) using lessons learned for sustaining expertise, (2) creating and maintaining quality instruction, and (3) developing structures and procedures to obtain the maximum potential from police training.

Chapter Four: The Police Responsibility to Community-Oriented Policing in a Diverse Society

Responsibility is the next tenet of professionalism receiving attention. It requires that the officer have an understanding of duty that is greater than service to oneself. The client of every profession is society. The police officer performs a service for the greater good much as doctors sustain public health, lawyers defend individual rights, and military personnel protect their citizenry. Such service to society implies that the professional police officer understands the social context in which he works.

Today this notion of service requires a community policing approach that recognizes social diversity. Every modern metropolitan area is a palette of rich demographic differences. The concepts underlying community policing and diversity awareness must therefore pervade the entire organization, including its training functions. This chapter details the need to integrate elements of community-oriented policing and diversity awareness models throughout training.

While corporateness addresses organizational *systems* and *procedures* that must support officer training, responsibility speaks more to the policing *philosophy* that a department chooses to advance. The systems of corporateness act to establish and maintain the philosophy of responsibility. Both systems and philosophy rely on the unique expertise that police officers provide to their clients.

Chapter Five: Developing Police Expertise

Expertise constitutes the third pillar of professionalism considered. Training develops and constantly hones the unique skills of a profession. While the LAPD Training Group is primarily responsible for formally developing the skills and expertise of Los Angeles officers, every leader and officer must unceasingly work to better himself and his colleagues as public servants. Department training in turn should not only help recruits become officers, but also constantly educate police at every echelon beyond their graduation from the academy.

As noted, we reviewed LAPD training in five subject areas: use of force, search and seizure, arrest procedures, community policing, and diversity awareness. We quickly realized that to fulfill the intent of the consent decree we could not treat these as separate entities. Nor can training treat them as independent, as they are inextricably interconnected parts of service on the streets. The five subject areas constitute a core set of skills that an ethical and effective police officer will regularly employ in combination. Our overriding recommendation in this area is that the LAPD training curriculum be integrated in a way that allows officers to realistically practice using all relevant skills and knowledge needed for effective police work, thus meeting current standards of excellence. Training in these areas cannot be effective if it simply entails a given number of stand-alone hours covering each of the five areas.

Expertise in these five areas demands more than physical adeptness. The professional officer is proficient in both technical skills (e.g., weapons proficiency, physical arrest procedures, and other topics frequently labeled as "tactical") and communication skills. The LAPD has a long history of excellence in technical proficiency, but our analysis indicates that most officers need more training in interpersonal and verbal communication skills than they currently receive. During interviews with Mayor James K. Hahn, Los Angeles City Council Public Safety Chair Cindy Miscikowski, members of the police commission, and community representatives, we repeatedly heard expressions of strong interest in greater interpersonal skills training for officers, especially those skills essential for deescalating conflicts. Effective communication is no less a vital "tactical" skill than are those related to weapons employment, expert driving, or other "hard" technical abilities. Good police officers are as skilled in communications as they are in "physical tactics." Police are frequently in the business of convincing people to do what they otherwise would not be inclined to do.[8] Officers must be adept at addressing all those in the "communication continuum," individuals ranging from those with whom they must work to resolve immediate issues to representatives of the mass media who will report or interpret their actions.

RESEARCH METHODOLOGY AND DATA ANALYSIS

In this section we detail the study methodology, describing the data collection processes as well as the analysis undertaken. The project team included RAND researchers, a community outreach consultant, and an expert panel of five police practitioners (see Appendix A). The RAND team contributed expertise in research design and the fields of law enforcement, education and training, operations research, sociology, psychology, and organizational behavior. The community outreach consultant added significant local knowledge regarding the history of police-community relations in Los Angeles and provided contacts with important community leaders and elected officials. The expert panel shared from their extensive experience in policing throughout the process. The panelists participated in problem analysis, debated alternative solutions to training problems, and reviewed project materials.

The research team used a variety of methods to collect data for this effort. Most of the analysis was based on qualitative data, which was gathered from the following sources:

---

[8]Ibid.

- literature reviews in the areas of adult and police education, policing, use of force, search and seizure, arrest procedures, community policing, and diversity awareness

- a case study survey of best practices in the field of policing, both domestic and international

- a review of written course documents, Department policies, and protocols

- observations of training instruction sessions

- focus group sessions with police department personnel

- interviews with police managers, elected officials, and community members.

The authors engaged in a process called "theory building through case analysis."[9] Such a process is used when there is no existing theory that sufficiently covers all aspects of the field under consideration. Our examination included police training, law enforcement operations, legal and community standards, and the specific mandates of the consent decree. There was no single applicable overarching theory. Thus, we engaged in theory building through our data collection and analytical efforts. Theory building is an iterative process: Gather data, examine data, develop a theory that appears to fit the data, and then validate and refine the theory through further data gathering and analysis. In this process, data collection and analysis are interwoven procedures.[10] Field testing of the recommendations made herein was not possible given study time constraints.

The activities inherent in the analysis that underlies this study were as follows.

Literature Reviews

The research team reviewed academic and practitioner literature in the areas of adult and police education, policing, use of force, search

---

[9]Eisenhardt, 1989, p. 532.

[10]Strauss and Corbin, 1990, p. 280.

and seizure, arrest procedures, community policing, and diversity awareness. Results from the literature reviews informed the development of the curriculum assessment instrument (Appendix B), and laid an important foundation for understanding the data collected at the LAPD. Together with the case studies, the literature reviews established that valuable material in specific subject areas exists, but that there are two fundamental gaps in the knowledge base of the field. One is the failure to meaningfully measure outcomes from police training. It is behavioral outcomes—actions of officers in the field—that are ultimately of interest to police educators. Yet work in this area is in its early stages. It cannot be said with certainty what kind of training works best for police. We are instead required to extrapolate from more general educational sources as well as to gather knowledge from related disciplines, such as the military.

Case Studies

The second fundamental gap in knowledge in the field was highlighted by both literature reviews and case studies. These two tools were used to survey the state of the art in policing. Sources indicated that breaking the study's topic areas into isolated parts is unsatisfactory. There is excellent writing on specific subject areas, for example in the area of use of force. Generally speaking, however, each topic is handled discretely and is not tied to other topics and, further, not tied to training. There are some exceptions, but the comprehensive attempt that this study represents is among the first of its kind.

Yet respondents in the case study interviews made clear the integrated nature of the research areas and demonstrated how the relevant issues are interwoven throughout police operations. For instance, when discussing use-of-force training, sources inevitably moved to discussion of review boards, risk management, and public perception, indicating that it is artificial to speak strictly of training. We were left in the gap between segmented literature and the reality of police operations, which is that all these issues are at play all the time. To continue in a segmented fashion, making audit-type recommendations, seemed to us to add only marginal value and perhaps even detract from the reform efforts of the Department, tying it to soon-to-be-obsolete and ill-fitting mandates.

Instead, this paradox of overly discrete versus overly holistic approaches seemed to demand an organizing principle. An organizing principle speaks not to a goal (for instance of crime control), it speaks to how that goal will be achieved. It provides operating rules. Small, seemingly insignificant decisions can be as readily guided by the principle as macro-level, comprehensive-change initiatives are. It distills the essence of not what a police officer is, but who he is, both as part of the organization and on an individual level, thereby allowing for coherent decisionmaking in any range of situations.

To identify the initial list of case study agencies, we used literature reviews, personal knowledge of researchers, and recommendations by the expert panel members. Police agencies in 20 jurisdictions were evaluated for the applicability of their experiences to the challenges confronting the LAPD. The thirteen sites ultimately selected for in-depth review were metropolitan areas with particularly relevant lessons for use of force, search and seizure, arrest procedures, community policing, and diversity awareness (see Appendix J).

Written Curriculum Review and Classroom Observation

Simultaneous to the early work of the literature reviews and case study interviews, we began our foray into the classrooms and written materials of the LAPD. What we saw quickly corroborated our preliminary sense of a missing piece. Individual instructors and individual courses carefully described specific, technical matters. Yet, confusion in classroom discussions was evident. Students were having difficulty understanding how each segment related to another, much less how to apply them to a real-life situation. Fortunately, this was not true across the board. Some curricula and instructors deliberately interwove material and demanded synthesis and judgments from students. Yet, in general, there were important gaps between classroom learning and application in the field and transfer of skills across subject areas.

Adding to this issue, many instructors discussed their own philosophy or experiences rather than offering guides by which an LAPD officer should make a decision (e.g., "LAPD officers are public servants" or "the LAPD leadership does not feel that the ends justify the means"—how would these values guide daily work?). Some form of ethos was certainly being transmitted, but it often varied among instructors and courses. These inconsistencies seemed to support a culture of individual decisionmaking, a culture that could, at its crudest level, pose a liability problem for the Department.

The corroborated findings from these various sources gave rise to the overarching recommendation: The LAPD should adopt a new concept of professionalism in order to

- provide a construct that lends coherency to its training

- establish a basis for police officer standards of performance and conduct.

The classroom observations and written curriculum review provided a rich source of data for more specific recommendations as well. Our review of LAPD written materials included recruit academy courses in the five areas of interest as well as those covering the topics of ethics, professionalism, and LAPD history (see Appendixes E and F). Reviews of material pertaining to continuing education training (also called in-service training) again included the five areas noted in the consent decree, as did our reviews of the Continuing Education Delivery Plan (CEDP), values, ethics, supervision, instructor development, and field training. Examination of roll-call training also focused on the five consent decree areas. Finally, the research team reviewed the LAPD manual, Department policies, management papers, training bulletins, and various review board reports and findings for relevant insights. Written material and classroom observation data were entered into an Access database for purposes of analysis of summary statistics.

Classroom observations were a critical source of data. We observed 50 percent of the courses for which we conducted written material reviews. The classes observed were selected based on relevance to the topics of consent decree interest and "snowball sampling" (i.e., questions and insights from initial observations precipitated reviews of additional courses). Together this entailed observations of 25 courses at an average observation length of more than two hours per class. Here again the assessment instrument was used to examine courses, and data were entered into the Access database. Table 1.1 summarizes classroom observations as a percentage of the written materials reviewed in each primary category.

Table 1.1

**Classroom Observations As a Percentage of the
Written Materials Reviewed**

Classroom Observation Categories	Observations[a]
Recruit	44%
Continuing education	73%
Command staff	100%
Roll call	12%

[a]Observations are a percentage of written materials reviewed (i.e., the number of courses observed divided by the number of courses for which written materials were reviewed).

NOTES: Twenty-five courses were observed. The average observation length was over two hours, adding up to more than 50 hours of classroom observation.

The computer database allowed us to tally summary statistics about such items as types of teaching techniques used in a course. However, most of our data was qualitative, that is, things that cannot be counted. We therefore supplemented the brief statistical analysis with the in-depth process of theory building described above. We laid the groundwork for the theory building through an intermediary analysis of our course reviews, both written and observed. Appendix L summarizes major findings from this portion of our work. It is derived from the categories of inquiry in the assessment instrument. The categories common across topic areas included

* stated class objectives

* instructional style

* learning setting

* written curriculum quality

* adequacy of resources.

The reviews and observations further investigated the following specific elements of course content

* performance expectations

* individual accountability/responsibility

* integration of Department values/context/policies/mandates

- incorporation of a police professional ethic
- use of the professional ethic to establish context during training
- incorporation of community policing and diversity
- use of community policing/diversity to establish context
- tactical skills
- legal standards and definitions
- coverage of current topic-specific issues (e.g., changing demographics in Los Angeles)
- use of decisionmaking models appropriate to the topic (e.g., the use-of-force continuum)
- supervisor accountability/responsibility.

Police Focus Groups

Focus groups help to explore why people feel a certain way and provide insights into seemingly conflicting opinions, adding richness to other data collection efforts.[11] In the late fall of 2002, we held focus groups sessions with a total of 35 participants. We stratified these groups by function and rank. The facilitators worked from customized scripts that were adapted from the individual interview instrument. (See Appendix D.) We paired a note taker with a facilitator in each session and attempted to safeguard participants by assuring them that comments made in the session would not be attributed to individuals, but only to groups.

It is important to introduce a caveat for our focus group findings. First, the focus group sample was small in comparison to the size of the Department. Second, it was not selected randomly, as a result of causes beyond the researchers' control. We therefore cannot legitimately generalize findings from this group to the broader population of officers. We instead limited ourselves to drawing reasonable inferences and insights.

---

[11] Unpublished RAND research by Margaret C. Harrell, on selective qualitative research methods.

Focus group discussions were used to gather data. Each group focused on a different aspect of the training process (see Table 1.2):

- Training coordinators discussed in-service instruction and the tension between demands for centralized and decentralized training.

- Senior lead officers described community policing training and its implementation within the Department.

- Training group sergeants and lieutenants provided insights on the adequacy and effectiveness of current training methods, curriculum development, and instructor delivery.

- Probationers (officers with less than one year since academy graduation) described their perceptions of classroom and field training, effectiveness of instructors, and their level of preparation upon leaving the academy.

- Field training officers (FTOs) also discussed the distinctions between classroom and field training, levels of effectiveness among FTOs, and FTO training needs.

Interviews

Our final method of data collection was a series of individual interviews with police managers, elected officials, and community members (interviewees are listed in Appendix C). We conducted 25 of these interviews throughout the fall of 2002. The interviews were semi-structured. That is, we had an interview guide that was adapted to suit each situation. Conversations were not limited to the questions listed in Appendix D. The guide was pilot tested for inter-rater reliability (to determine whether interviewers asked questions in a consistent manner). Individuals who desired confidentiality were assured it.

Interviewees were selected for their expert knowledge and opinion. Individuals were identified by the research team, and none of the interviews was mandatory. Respondents were identified as key to this study by virtue of their positions in the community, city government,

Table 1.2

LAPD Focus Groups

Focus Group	Area of Interest	Major Themes
Training coordinators	Training delivery for in-service curriculum; centralized and decentralized needs	Not routinely asked for input on what is used for training or how it's delivered. Not asked about divisional needs for training. Asked to do many different tasks beyond "real" responsibilities. Were not handling such issues as 4th Amendment (search), false arrest, and use of force well when decentralized—could see need for centralizing training in these areas. In roll calls, think the training scenario should be acted out instead of just read.
Senior lead officers	Training for community-oriented policing (CP) and quality of life concerns; adequacy and effectiveness of field and in-service training	Only officers serve in community policing capacity. Think that the Department should emphasize CP to patrol officers. Believe that every captain runs division differently. May be pulled off CP to handle other duties. Taught CP and problem solving by their peers, not taught formally. Felt common in LAPD to be put on job without experience or training.
Training group sergeants and lieutenants	Adequacy and effectiveness of current training methods; curriculum development and delivery	Have added "drop-in" scenarios on all five recommended areas to recruit training. Think that each police officer 3 (senior) should spend one year as a field training officer (FTO) before being eligible to "go inside." Think that people should be moved through the training group—too many make a career of it. Like the British model—police do no classroom work, all scenario. Think the ride-along period should be extended to a month.

Table 1.2—Continued

Focus Group	Area of Interest	Major Themes
Probationers	Classroom versus field training; levels of effectiveness among instructors; level of preparation upon leaving academy	Disappointed with the lack of rigor in the training program at the academy, expected it to be harder than it was.
		Believe there is a "war out there" and wanted to be trained for it.
		Wanted more realistic and tougher training to "weed out" the weak or unsafe.
		Recommended ride-alongs earlier in process to give a better idea of what police work is like.
		Did not feel they left the academy with an LAPD "culture."
		Told by FTOs to forget the academy training—real training starts in the field.
Field training officers	Classroom versus field training; levels of effectiveness among FTOs; training needs of FTOs	Think that recruits do not receive enough training in real-life situations.
		Believe training should be more reflective of what is faced in the field.
		Believe that tactics training is still good but is affected by liability concerns; officer safety can be compromised (officers more likely to get hit first).
		See a disconnect between the FTO program and academy training—do not know what is being taught; have to ask recruits what they learned.
		Since FTO training only occurred once, no clear message heard yet from the Department on the role of the FTO.

and the LAPD. Additionally, throughout our work, in interviews, focus groups, and classroom observation, the research team made an effort to include individuals of diverse backgrounds.

Interview and focus group data were both analyzed. Interviews, used predominantly for background information, were summarized. Focus groups, used for data gathering, were informally coded to identify major themes and areas of convergence or discord.

Recommendations

As described above, theory building is an iterative process. In this study, RAND was able to complete all the steps of theory building except for the testing of the model. This is an important step, and its omission is not insignificant. As researchers, we hope for the opportunity to complete the process. However, we necessarily limited our inquiry because of external constraints. We are also assured that the models we used are based on theories grounded in the training and education fields.

This process of analysis led to identification of findings and recommendations. Above, we addressed the genesis of the overarching theme of a redefined professionalism. We similarly derived the primary recommendations (as well as the supporting recommendations) from shortfalls identified during our data collection and analysis. At least three data sources pointed to each of the primary recommendations. Generally, the expertise that team members brought to the project together with all data sources established each piece of evidence.

A brief note on each of the five primary recommendations follows. (See Appendix M for a complete list of our primary and supporting recommendations.)

Establish an LAPD Lessons-Learned Program

This recommendation derives from heterogeneous sources within and outside of the LAPD. Many businesses today have learned the value of becoming learning organizations and of developing strong knowledge management capabilities.[12] LAPD officials note that structural and cultural divisions among various units of the Department sometimes prevent the timely flow of information from the field to training and the reverse. Further, risk management and liability concerns support the need for a concrete effort to learn from previous actions.

Introduce and Maintain Consistently High Quality Throughout Every Aspect of LAPD Training

This finding addresses curriculum development, instructor quality, and assessment of learning. While the LAPD has undertaken training reform and has instituted some quality control initiatives, inconsistency of quality across curricula and instructors remains. The data that lead to this conclusion include classroom observation, document review, interviews with police personnel, and focus group responses.

Each reviewer of curriculum and observer of class sessions noted the inconsistency of training in his field notes. While there are individual examples of excellence, the inconsistencies were discovered across recruit, in-service, and management training, as well as across subject areas, indicating a need for improved overall quality control. Finally, this finding was also identified more than ten years ago in the Christopher Commission report. The LAPD continues to attempt to sufficiently revise its training protocols.

Restructure the LAPD Training Group to Allow the Centralization of Planning; Instructor Qualification, Evaluation, and Learning Retention; and More Efficient Use of Resources

This finding arose predominantly through identification by mid- and senior-level leadership in the LAPD. RAND was asked to suggest ways in which the training group might reorganize its functions so as to work more effectively. The request was bolstered by results from the focus groups as well as field observations about the nature and

---

[12]See work by Peter Senge and Jeffrey Pfeffer.

structure of the various training functions. Specifically, the division between recruit and in-service training functions, the unclear role and chain of command of training coordinators, and the manner in which roll-call curriculum was developed and delivered were all major points noted by interview respondents as well as researcher observation.

Integrate Elements of Community-Oriented Policing and Diversity Awareness Training Models Throughout LAPD Training

The isolated, segregated nature of community policing training was apparent from every data source. Elected officials and community members expressed desires to see more meaningful community engagement and partnership. Meanwhile, many Department personnel struggled to define what community policing is, much less to provide examples of how it is implemented. Case studies and literature reviews underlined that community policing is a department-wide endeavor. It is not a discrete task during the activity of policing and, therefore, cannot be handled as a discrete part of training.

Develop Training on Use of Force, Search and Seizure, and Arrest Procedures That Meets Current Standards of Excellence

This recommendation was heavily informed by curriculum review, classroom observation, and focus group responses. Some courses in these areas follow best practices in learning principles and some do not. Current training in these areas ranges from high quality to that needing substantial improvement, as understood by training experts, students of the courses, and community members and elected officials who see the translation to behavior in the field. While we did not measure student outcomes (how much officers learned and how they applied that learning in the field), classroom observations and focus group/interview responses indicated that students were not grasping the underlying principles of use of force, search and seizure, and arrest policies, or the interrelatedness of these three topic areas together and with community policing and diversity awareness.

NOTES

The authors ask readers to note the following four issues:

- *Gender pronouns.* We have chosen to use the male pronoun to avoid complicated and grammatically incorrect alternatives to gender specificity. We encourage the reader to see these notations as inclusive of individuals of both sexes, whether among LAPD officers or Los Angeles community members. The use of the male pronoun is not intended to imply that policing is a male profession.

- *Policing/law enforcement.* We understand that "policing" and "law enforcement" are not synonyms. We are keenly aware that the work of police officers is greater than simply enforcing the law. We have nonetheless chosen to use the terms interchangeably to avoid bludgeoning readers with overuse of either term.

- *Training/education.* We also acknowledge that "training" and "education" are not synonymous. Some in the field of professional development feel that the term "training" is limiting and is perhaps not appropriate when applied to human development. Others counter that training is more encompassing and involves greater internalization than does the concept of "education." The term "training" is substantially used in police work and is a well understood and accepted term. Good training includes education; education of police officers includes training. We use these terms interchangeably.

- *Access.* Finally, we make an administrative note: Throughout all of our data collection efforts, LAPD personnel provided complete access to individuals, groups, classrooms, and precincts. We experienced no resistance to our requests.

Chapter Two

THE LUSTER IN THE BADGE: LAW ENFORCEMENT
PROFESSIONALISM AND THE LAPD

At first glance, it might seem that there is little to logically link police instruction on use of force, search and seizure, arrest procedures, community policing, and diversity awareness. Why, for example, should an academy integrate community-policing concerns with instruction regarding basic arrest techniques? How does it serve the police department or the public to consider demographic characteristics when teaching use-of-force procedures? Does providing equal service to all mean that identical procedures have to be employed for every search, regardless of a person's gender, religion, race, ability to communicate, or handicaps? The answers to these and similar questions are found in the following discussion of a revised concept of law enforcement professionalism, which is used in the remainder of this study.

"Professionalism" as introduced in this chapter inherently incorporates many concepts already familiar to dedicated police officers. The guidelines provided by the LAPD's core values and management principles (see Appendixes E and F) are an example—they rest on the same moral foundation that underlies any profession. A police department that looks to ethics and integrity as touchstones for judgment and service inherently shares elements of a professional approach. We have chosen professionalism as the underpinning for this study because it encompasses and synthesizes all the good elements that these other factors include. In addition, policing is only one of many vocations that can qualify as a profession. Law enforcement personnel also share important characteristics with these other entities while being in their own sense unique. The construct of professionalism provides a common context for learning from other vocations that serve the public while at the same time emphasizing the special attributes that make police unlike any other group of people in the world.

WHAT DOES IT MEAN TO SERVE WITH THE LAPD?

> It is the mission of the Los Angeles Police Department to safeguard the lives and property of the people we serve, to reduce the incidence and fear of crime, and to enhance public safety while working with the diverse communities to improve their quality of life. Our mandate is to do so with honor and integrity, while at all times conducting ourselves with the highest ethical standards to maintain public confidence (LAPD, 2003b).

The above is the mission, the "specific task with which a person or group is charged," that establishes the reason the Los Angeles Police Department exists and why its officers are vested with the authority inherent in being law enforcement officials.[1] It is a responsibility of all members of the LAPD to "safeguard the lives and property of the people [they] serve" and to do so "with honor and integrity, while at all times conducting [them]selves with the highest ethical standards to maintain public confidence." The mission establishes service as the foundation of the department's duties, a service guided by shared standards of a supreme caliber.

This mission specifies "what" the officers of the LAPD are to do; the Department's statements of its core values and principles lend insights into "how" that primary task is to be accomplished. The principles begin by addressing how police officers are to safeguard lives and property. They are to enforce the law, but not just any law (there are various codes worldwide, many designed to subjugate or control rather than protect those to whom they apply). Department principles explain that officers' application of the law must be "within a legal spirit which was so clearly set forth by the framers of the Bill of Rights."[2] The laws that members of the LAPD enforce are therefore in the spirit of guaranteeing the Fourth Amendment's "right of the

---

[1] *Merriam Webster's Collegiate Dictionary*, 10th ed., s.v. "mission," 1993.

[2] LAPD, 2003c.

people to be secure in their persons, houses, papers, and effects, against unreasonable searches and seizures" and other fundamental rights and freedoms. Further, officers are not to

> enforce any law which shall abridge the privileges or immunities of citizens of the United States; nor shall [they] deprive any person of life, liberty, or property, without due process of law; nor deny to any person within its jurisdiction the equal protection of the laws[3]

as held sacred in the Fourteenth Amendment. The people whose lives and property the LAPD safeguards include the same individuals and groups that the Bill of Rights champions.

The Department principles and core values draw directly on these Constitutional guarantees. They do so "by constantly demonstrating absolutely impartial service to the law" while remembering that "the police are the only members of the public who are paid to give full-time attention to duties which are incumbent on every citizen in the interest of community welfare" (LAPD, 2003c). The LAPD police officer is to conduct this service within the bounds of proper authority, "never appear[ing] to usurp the powers of the judiciary" (LAPD, 2003c) and serving all citizens "with equal dedication" (LAPD, 2003e). The police are to unfailingly display "a reverence for the legal rights of our fellow citizens and a reverence for the law itself" (LAPD, 2003c). Police serve "fellow citizens." The rights they protect are as much their own as they are those for whom they serve. As George Washington wrote, "when we assumed the soldier we did not lay aside the citizen."[4] The same is true for law enforcement officers.

Accomplishing the LAPD mission while meeting Department standards requires considerable expertise. It is because the police officer possesses special education and experience that he is entrusted with the responsibility to pay "full-time attention to the duties that are incumbent on every citizen" (LAPD, 2003c). Officers are to develop and maintain this expertise that is unique to them alone. No other group of individuals is so empowered and bears this burden. The LAPD officer's way of life is one of shared values and responsibility to

---

[3]*U.S. Constitution,* 2003, amend. 14.

[4]This quotation appears on the amphitheater immediately behind the Tomb of the Unknown Soldier in Arlington Cemetery.

ensure that all police maintain the standards associated with those values.

Service to the public, special skills and a unique expertise, and the obligation to maintain standards based on shared values are characteristics of a profession. Can it be legitimately said that law enforcement officers, in particular those of the Los Angeles Police Department, belong to a profession and are themselves, individually, professionals? The answer is an important one. While fellow citizens grant to professionals considerable prestige and respect, membership in a profession also demands the acceptance of responsibilities well beyond those of a mere jobholder. The individual who serves only for wages or self-gratification does not qualify for the status of a professional. A professional's work is more akin to a calling than an occupation, a calling that demands full-time dedication of his professional life, service to the public, and a lifetime commitment to the profession's standards.

WHAT IS A PROFESSION?

Numerous books have been written on professionalism and professional organizations. Two that consider military professionalism also highlight ways in which to consider law enforcement as a profession.

Allan Millett identifies six definitive elements of any profession:

- The occupation is a full-time and stable job, serving continuing societal needs;
- The occupation is regarded as a lifelong calling by the practitioners, who identify themselves personally with their job subculture;
- The occupation is organized to control performance standards and recruitment;
- The occupation requires formal, theoretical education;
- The occupation has a service orientation in which loyalty to standards of competence and loyalty to clients' needs are paramount;

- The occupation is granted a great deal of collective autonomy by the society it serves, presumably because the practitioners have proven their high ethical standards and trustworthiness.[5]

Millett notes that "professional" status encourages its holders to behave in a more socially responsible manner. At the same time, there is considerable freedom and responsibility granted to individuals who make this sacrifice. They

> create their own ethical codes; establish their own educational system; recruit their own members; and maintain a unique occupational culture on the assumptions that the professional's services represent social good, that the monopoly conditions that the professional prefers represent human progress . . . . The professional's competency will be judged by his peers, and his conduct will be determined by the norms of his profession. He will not abuse society's faith in his skill by ignoring either his client's needs or the regulating judgment of his colleagues. . . . the professional's relative freedom is conditional and ultimately depends on continuous social approval. Without constant self-policing and task success, a profession can narrow its own freedom and destroy public trust as rapidly as it gained its relative autonomy.[6]

Professional status is conditional upon members maintaining their standards through self-policing. That does not mean that professions will not suffer lapses by their members. The My Lai massacres of the Vietnam War and more recent cases of child molestation by clergy provide ample evidence that they do. Such incidents place the onus of recovering professional status squarely on its members, those collectively responsible for the initial dereliction.

Samuel P. Huntington defines professionalism based on the three "distinguishing characteristics": corporateness, responsibility, and expertise. He defines each of these as follows (Huntington, 1957, pp. 8–10, 15):

---

[5]Millett, 1977, p. 2.
[6]Ibid., p. 3.

Corporateness

The members of a profession share a sense of organic unity and consciousness of themselves as a group apart from laymen. This collective sense has its origins in the lengthy discipline and training necessary for professional competence, the common bond of work, and the sharing of a unique social responsibility . . . . Entrance into this unit is restricted to those with the requisite education and training and is usually permitted only at the lowest level of professional competence.

Responsibility

The professional man is a practicing expert, working in a social context, and performing a service, such as the promotion of health, education, or justice, which is essential to the functioning of society. The client of every profession is society, individually or collectively. . . . Financial remuneration cannot be the primary aim of the professional man. . . . The profession [is] a moral unit positing certain values and ideals which guide its members in their dealings with laymen. This guide may be a set of unwritten norms transmitted through the professional educational system or it may be codified into written canons of professional ethics.

Expertise

The professional man is an expert with specialized knowledge and skill in a significant field of human endeavor. His expertise is acquired only by prolonged education and experience. It is the basis of objective standards of professional competence.

Like Millett, Huntington recognizes that professionalism is a goal, because "no vocation, not even medicine or law, has all the characteristics of the ideal professional type."[7] That in no way excuses any member of the profession from doing his utmost to gain and maintain the prescribed standards. It does allow that the occasional

---

[7]Huntington, 1957, p. 11.

member of the profession will falter and that other members will have to repair the resulting loss in public confidence.

Both authors' definitions share many characteristics. They present discussions in the context of the military, but each emphasizes that their definition of a profession applies to any vocation that meets the specified qualifications. Either man's professional tenets could be adopted for use in this study without loss of understanding. Millett is more explicit, using six characteristics to articulate that which separates the professional from others in a workforce. Huntington exercises greater conciseness, a brevity that is nonetheless no less inclusive or demanding than Millett's. The following adopts this more concise of the two as the primary vehicle for analysis, incorporating pertinent elements of Millett's conceptualization where they improve understanding of the demands professional status poses for the City of Los Angeles police officer.

IS LAW ENFORCEMENT A PROFESSION?

It would appear obvious at first glance that law enforcement has a legitimate claim to professional status. Regarding corporateness, law enforcement officers are bonded by a cooperative sense of union based on shared expectations and responsibilities. The responsibility for self-policing has always been and must always be an integral part of senior police officers' charters. Entrusted with greater authority, they have both a professional and bureaucratic dictate to enforce standards. But a profession cannot surrender the responsibility for internal policing solely to those of higher rank. Any "code of silence" notwithstanding, a police officer failing to address shortfalls in other members of his vocation fails in his duties. Depending on the severity of the shortfall, he may be, and should be, liable to punishment and banishment from his force.

Police officers also have a broad responsibility to society—their client. They perform a service that is essential to its functioning. Pay is of course important, and nobody expects a professional not to receive fair compensation for his services. Financial remuneration, however, should no more be the primary motivation for assuming the status of a police officer than it is for a doctor practicing medicine or a military officer leading the nation's youth in peace or war.

With regard to the third tenet, police officers clearly have special expertise. They receive specialized training and are expected to maintain a combination of physical, communications, and diplomatic skills unique to their vocation. Legislators make law. Judges and lawyers interpret and deal with alleged and actual breaches of the law. Only police officers assume a full-time occupational responsibility to enforce the law or interrupt the processes that cause such breaches. They do so with training that begins at an academy and continues throughout their careers. That training delineates professional standards that an officer must follow, including those pertaining to restraint when using force, adherence to the spirit and letter of the law, and control in exercising the formal and informal authority inherent in status as a police officer.

While the above demonstrates that police work incorporates elements of corporateness, responsibility, and expertise, there are reasonable arguments against conferring professional status on the police. Some, for example, argue that personnel who might have to kill in pursuit of their responsibilities cannot be professionals, because they do not serve the best interests of all in the society that they are to serve.[8] Police must sometimes use deadly force in fulfilling their duties. Nevertheless, just as the military ultimately seeks to maintain peace and stability and must sometimes use lethal force, so do police desire to maintain a safe environment free of crime. That the greater number are protected through the occasional unfortunate demise of a threatening few certainly does not preclude the police officer from professional status as long as the application of force remains within the constraints of acceptable standards.

Some argue that police officers are "subsumed within a vast government bureaucracy" and therefore lack "the autonomy and interaction with a bona fide clientele enjoyed by the traditional professions" such as the clergy, doctors, or lawyers.[9] The argument would be persuasive if professional status were only granted to those perfectly attaining the condition of self-regulation. Government mandates, however, influence many aspects of medicine, law, and any modern

---

[8]Matthews, 1994, p. 18.

[9]Ibid. The comments are made with respect to the military but apply no less to police forces.

profession. All are answerable to regulation and the rule of law. External bureaucratic oversight should not preclude attainment of professional standing.

Another question is of self-perception. Self-perception is critical to professionalism. No vocation can be considered professional if its members do not accept the collective responsibility to maintain a specialized expertise, to limit membership to those with the requisite skills and who adhere to established standards, and to have a primary motivation of serving society. It is therefore pertinent to ask whether police officers themselves view their work as a profession.

The answer is a mixed one. Several retired senior police leaders with whom the authors discussed the issue thought it infeasible, claiming that the officer on the street was too focused on a steady job and its pay to qualify as a professional. LAPD Police Chief William J. Bratton's belief that policing is a profession is evident in his previously cited quotation. Evidence from other LAPD officers varies. Police probationers showed limited understanding of professional responsibilities but recognized that the academy sought to instill desirable traits in recruits and to define acceptable standards of performance. None of the probationers interviewed cited a desire to serve the community when asked why they joined the force, nor did any of the field-training officers whom we interviewed. Their predominant motivations were, in fact, pay and the need to find a job.[10] Yet nearly all students in a Department watch-commander course cited a desire "to help people" as the primary reason for becoming police officers.

The Department does seek to instill the tenets of professionalism in its training. Recruit Training Program Learning Domain #31 on "Custody," for example, emphasizes values such as "integrity in all we say and do," "quality through continuous improvement," "respect for people," "reverence for the law," and "service to our community." In recognition of a need to better interact with those served, the curriculum also cites an objective of "reestablish[ing] partnership with community." Specific guidance includes "protecting the statutory and Constitutional rights of the arrested person while they are in the officer's charge" and recognition that "a

---

[10]LAPD probationers focus group and FTO focus group notes, December 14, 2002.

peace officer that shows a callous disregard for an arrested person's safety can be subjected to departmental discipline (up to and including termination)." The lesson goes on to include discussions of specific Bill of Rights protections and responsibilities inherent in the "special position of trust" given to peace officers based on "their authority over others."[11]

The evidence as to whether LAPD officers consider themselves to be "professionals" is contradictory. Those writing of the broader law enforcement profession are less ambivalent. The mid-20th century saw considerable efforts to establish a professional policing model that included identification of principles (or standards) as well as providing police departments some level of independence from politics, ensuring satisfactory officer training and discipline, and impartiality in enforcing the law.[12] The LAPD at that time represented the model of such a professional force while under the oversight of Chief William H. Parker. The ideal was a situation in which police corruption was controlled via the selection of qualified candidates for police duties and internal handling of Department problems.[13] The popular form of this ideal was *Dragnet* (Joe Friday and his characteristic, "Just the facts") in which the police professional was honest, tough, and technically proficient. While missing nuances, the depiction of a technically proficient force that attempted to maintain complete objectivity during interactions with the public was not far from reality.

But Joe Friday would fail to qualify as a professional police officer in Los Angeles today. His integrity and dedication deserve no less respect now than they did 50 years ago, but his overly reserved manner should, deservedly, be relegated to a past age. Police standards have evolved. Police professionalism now demands expertise and an understanding of the community in many ways not previously appreciated. Law enforcement officers today seek not only to deal with crimes already committed but to prevent crimes by addressing the issues that underlie them. "By-the-book" adherence to regulations has been replaced by increased reliance on innovation, initiative,

---

[11]LAPD, revised 2001a.

[12]Fyfe et al., 1997, p. 15.

[13]Walker, Archbold, and Herbst, 2002.

and expertise in interpersonal interactions more akin to August Vollmer's concept of policing than the reform-based organizations that resulted from a misapplication of his principles (see Kelling and Coles, 1996, p. 75). Herman Goldstein, a scholar and longtime student of policing, notes that expanded standards for policing now require officers to

- assist those who cannot care for themselves: the intoxicated, the addicted, the mentally ill, the physically disabled, the old, and the young
- resolve conflict, whether it be between individuals [or] groups of individuals
- identify problems that have the potential for becoming more serious problems for the individual citizen, the police, or for government
- create and maintain a feeling of security in the community.[14]

Bratton and Andrews add support for a post-reform concept of policing, noting that now "police work is by nature decentralized and discretionary."[15]

In sum, the question of whether law enforcement qualifies as a profession might best be answered by considering two separate questions. First, can law enforcement qualify as a profession? There appears to be ample evidence that it can. Second, can the LAPD be a professional force? It was considered so in the mid-20th century, albeit by standards that no longer apply (and that in truth failed to meet even the definition of professionalism at the time). We now turn to evidence regarding whether it can be so considered today.

CAN THE LAPD BE A PROFESSIONAL FORCE?

The LAPD has made efforts to become a professional force as the term is currently understood in policing. There is room for improvement, and it is the charter of this study to consider how that can be brought about in training involving use of force, search and

---

[14]Herman Goldstein, *Policing a Free Society*, Cambridge, Mass.: Ballinger, 1977, p. 35, as quoted in Fyfe et al., 1997, p. 37.

[15]Bratton and Andrews, 1999, p. 14.

seizure, arrest procedures, community policing, and diversity aware-ness. The solutions must have a Department-wide perspective. Au-thors Kelling and Stewart note that the successful implementation of police professionalism today requires "major changes in the training of police officers, supervisors, and managers, as well as in staffing, organization, and administration of police departments."[16]

The following pages address the nature of these necessary changes as they pertain to training the men and women of the LAPD. To the question "Is the Los Angeles Police Department a professional law enforcement organization?" the evidence in too many ways supports a negative response. "Can the LAPD be a professional force?" Evi-dence seems to support an affirmative answer, but individual and collective dedication to making the necessary changes is necessary to get there from here.

GETTING THERE FROM HERE

An LAPD effort to achieve professional status is important only in the sense that it makes the organization a better servant of its clients, the people of Los Angeles. It is the purpose of this study to determine how the Department can achieve that end through the medium of training the force so that it is more proficient in the five areas of con-cern. Huntington's tenets of professionalism—corporateness, re-sponsibility, and expertise—provide a vehicle to better understand what is necessary to meet that purpose. Those tenets, in fact profes-sionalism itself, provide a foundation essential to successful training and implementation of areas of use of force, search and seizure, ar-rest procedures, community policing, and diversity awareness. Suc-cess in attaining professionalism demands commitment to public service, requisite expertise throughout the Department, and the real-ization that fellow officers have a responsibility to assist their col-leagues when situations stress the patience of even the best. Figure 2.1, each element of which will be explained in detail in the pages that follow, helps to portray how the three tenets can assist in the de-velopment and execution of LAPD training. The objective of that training is to better prepare law enforcement officers for the task of

---

[16]Fyfe et al., 1997, p. 23.

RAND *MR1745-2.1*

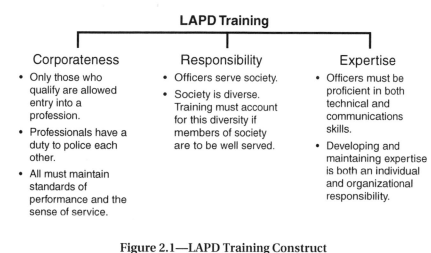

Figure 2.1—LAPD Training Construct

meeting the demands inherent in daily accomplishment of the Department's mission.

It has been noted that there are those who believe that police are not and never will be professionals. These individuals see law enforcement officers as little more than wage laborers. Such doubters find it unconvincing that there are police officers who have the necessary expertise, will act to correct other officers' shortcomings, and are dedicated to public service. They consider those personnel demonstrating these abilities to be exceptional, outliers perhaps best considered as professionals without a profession. Many looking at the performance of the LAPD over the past two decades might agree. But neither the past nor the present need determine the state of the future. That every profession falls short of the ideal is established. That police officers could be professionals should certainly not be considered beyond the realm of the achievable. That there are already examples for others to follow is encouraging. That such status is a goal entirely suitable for these invaluable servants of the public as a whole seems unquestionable. As such the overarching recommendation of this study is the following:

The Los Angeles Police Department should adopt a concept of police professionalism that incorporates the tenets of corporateness, responsibility, and expertise as the mechanism for guiding the development and execution of its training, to include training in the areas of use of force, search and seizure, arrest procedures, community policing, and diversity awareness.

Chapter Three

CORPORATENESS

INTRODUCTION

> The members of a profession share a sense of organic unity and
> consciousness of themselves as a group apart from laymen. This
> collective sense has its origins in the lengthy discipline and training
> necessary for professional competence, the common bond of work,
> and the sharing of a unique social responsibility. . . . Entrance into
> this unit is restricted to those with the requisite education and
> training and is usually permitted only at the lowest level of profes-
> sional competence.

Samuel Huntington, 1957

The corporateness element of professionalism implicitly requires
adherence to and maintenance of standards, both at an individual
and institutional level. The requirement of professional standards
implies that there must be training regarding these standards; otherwise, there is no opportunity to inculcate the values and methods
of the profession. Furthermore, the training must not only transmit
the profession's ethos, it must do so in such a way that allows no
conflicting interpretations. Simply establishing accepted standards
is insufficient. The accepted standards must be communicated to
and enforced by LAPD officers.

Implementing the requisites of corporateness makes many demands
on an organization and its leadership. Despite personnel and bud-
getary resource constraints, recruitment and hiring must still strive

to attract the type of individual that will meet the standard of a professional LAPD officer. Existing hiring processes that may "select out" less desirable candidates rather than "select in" more desirable candidates require revision.[1] Recruiting should seek individuals wanting a professional career in law enforcement rather than simply a steady paycheck. It would be better for the LAPD to hire fewer officers of high quality than greater numbers whose performance undermines public confidence. Promotion criteria should be set to support current goals of police professionalism. Training at every level should consistently seek to build the expertise, sense of commitment, and understanding of collective responsibility that is the foundation for a professional law enforcement organization.

Three different issues related to corporateness can abet further development of a more professional force (and hence one more qualified to manage the challenges inherent in the five areas of concern in this study). These issues are

- integrating lessons learned in the field into Department training in order to maintain and improve skills

- ensuring that the training function consistently preserves standards of excellence across the force and in its instructors

- restructuring the LAPD training organization to allow for optimum performance.

---

[1]Assistant Chief James McDonnell, LAPD, interview by Estela Lopez and Barbara R. Panitch.

EVERY COP A TEACHER: A CALL FOR CREATING AN EFFECTIVE LESSONS-LEARNED PROGRAM

Primary Recommendation

Establish an LAPD lessons-learned program.

What is training? It is changing behavior.

William J. Bratton
City of Los Angeles Chief of Police
February 13, 2003

Lessons Learned and What They Offer the LAPD

A lessons-learned mechanism would have dual benefits in the area of community policing. Not only would it help senior lead officers and others to see how problems were addressed in another part of the city, it could provide the community link that is largely absent in training. Historically, residents have been the consumers of police services rather than contributors to the problem-solving process. There have been civilians working with officers who have done their share of the heavy lifting, but only the involved officers know this. A distribution avenue such as a lessons-learned center could ultimately result in modifications to training based on partnerships with the community.

Maintaining professional expertise is a continual process. Many professions require members to complete continuing education programs to maintain their standing. Other organizations hold periodic mandatory training sessions that focus on pertinent topics or require members to develop a personal reading program based on recommended readings focusing on the profession. Such programs seek to disseminate knowledge considered necessary for maintaining skills. A profession will stagnate, lapse in its expertise, or otherwise fail in its service to society if it does not constantly update the knowledge of its members.

Police organizations generally leave the discovery and teaching of new material to their training function and on-the-job experience. Only by exception, such as in the case of a fatal shooting involving an officer or a mishandled riot, do departments conduct investigations that result in dramatic training and policy changes. There is rarely a means in place for promoting the transmission of good practices among precincts or encouraging individual police officers to share innovative concepts. A valuable initiative can take months or years to gain recognition. When there is no mechanism in place to make an innovative officer's initiatives known to a wide audience, they can be lost entirely if he leaves the department.

We found little evidence of effective compilation and dissemination of lessons learned in the world of policing. Fortunately, there is an example from the military environment that provides a basis for study and adaptation. The U.S. Army historically suffered from problems in sharing lessons learned. The pressures of day-to-day operations meant that a unit developing means to overcome a new problem or enemy tactic would not typically share its experience unless leaders ensured that units were debriefed on return from missions. Even then the material would too often languish at a lower echelon or otherwise fail to progress up the chain of command and from there be disseminated to others in the field. Such failures cost lives.

The need for better passing of insights on to others in the organization repeatedly made itself evident. It surfaced during World War II and Korea and again in Vietnam. Units met the need in various ways. During the Vietnam War, for example, the 1st Cavalry Division collected field observations and took steps to ensure that such lessons were sent to those serving in the field. The division's school for soldiers newly arriving in the combat zone immediately introduced these field observations into its curriculum. Commands in Vietnam regularly submitted an "Operational Report—Lessons Learned" that spread the word regarding new discoveries and innovations by field soldiers.[2] Such reports served as an important source of the material used in the division school and passed to organizations in contact with the enemy.

---

[2]Glenn, 2000, p. 13.

The army found that it was also encountering problems in sharing peacetime lessons learned. In 1985, it therefore created the Center for Army Lessons Learned (CALL), the foremost center in the world for gathering information of value to its organization and making it available to those to whom it is of value. CALL collects lessons, observations, insights, and suggestions from the army's major combat training centers. It sends military and civilian analysts to theaters of operation to bring back information of value to the service as a whole. The organization also allows any soldier, anywhere, anytime, to provide his observations on how the army might better prepare for conflict. But collection is not enough. Any such program is worthless without distribution. CALL also sends instructor teams out to teach units in the field and provides its materials on a web site and in written form, sending particularly timely lessons directly to the service's top leadership and training centers.

Like the military, the police force must constantly learn and adapt. Changes in the law, equipment, and criminal behavior all require new skills and training. Most of these new skills requirements and training are identified through well-established mechanisms. Legislative liaisons or a department's legal personnel suggest adjustments based on changes to the law. Centralized police training standards are in part decided by outside entities such as Peace Officer Standards and Training (POST). Those responsible for bringing new equipment into a department either contract for training as part of the purchase or develop internal means of educating those who will employ the equipment in the field.

Other less routine needs for new training are not as easily identified. Innovations in one police department may take months or years to spread elsewhere. A member of the LAPD might recognize a shortcoming in a routine procedure and develop an innovative way to address it, but, without means to pass such innovations along, the idea will not spread beyond the few officers in direct contact with the innovator. Policing is a dynamic vocation; its environment, challenges, and capabilities are ever changing. Its education systems have to be equally dynamic in their ability to recognize and disseminate necessary change. There is need for a formal system of collecting, processing, and distributing lessons learned.

No police department can afford an organization like CALL, but neither can a department forsake the opportunity to teach its members lessons from those best qualified to understand their needs—fellow members of the police vocation. The following section reviews CALL operations further with an emphasis on determining how the LAPD can best take advantage of this educational methodology at a reasonable cost.

Supporting Recommendation

Assign the training group primary responsibility for the lessons-learned program.

Developing Lessons Learned

A "lesson learned" is one of "validated knowledge and experience derived from observation and historical study of training, exercises, and operations."[3] The initial objective in working with lessons learned is to determine what performance changes are necessary. Such changes "may result in either stopping something we have been doing, doing something differently . . . or doing something new that we have not done before."[4] Lessons learned complement training in bringing about desired change. Given the role they can fulfill in training, it is most appropriate to make the LAPD Training Group the repository for overseeing a lessons-learned program.

Developing lessons learned involves far more than simply collecting good ideas and passing them on to instructors. Lessons-learned submittals have to be screened by an individual with the expertise to recognize their value (if any) and relevance to ongoing or future operations. It may be feasible to assign lessons-learned collection responsibility to a single individual. However, that individual will have to be in contact with others possessing the necessary expertise and authority to determine how a lesson is best used and to whom it should be made available when he lacks that knowledge. These ad-

---

[3]Center for Army Lessons Learned, 2003.
[4]Ibid.

junct personnel can simply be points of contact—a specified member of the senior lead officers, gang unit, or narcotics division, for example. Their participation would be limited to corresponding with the primary lessons-learned manager via telephone or email in response to specific inquiries when their specialized expertise is necessary to evaluate a particular lessons-learned proposal. The following sections look at each of the components of the lessons-learned process in greater detail.

Identifying and Distributing Lessons Learned

Lessons-Learned Recipients. The purpose of establishing a system for collecting and distributing lessons learned is to enhance LAPD officers' expertise and, thereby, the quality of their service to the people of Los Angeles. Some of its products will be distributed to instructors for their use in courses. Others might be distributed more broadly to LAPD officers, while still others should be shared with law enforcement officers in other departments.

Supporting Recommendation

Establish and maintain lessons-learned links with other police departments and law enforcement agencies.

Assigning responsibility for a lessons-learned program to the training group gives the LAPD the opportunity to reach a broad number of officers. Some lessons might best be taught in only a single academy class or continuing education course; others may have broader application. The training group will need to synchronize the introduction of new material so that it is presented consistently at academy, continuing education, and roll-call sessions in a form suitable for each audience. In some cases, lessons will simply be one-time notices brought to the Department's attention. In other cases, lessons will become long-standing elements in particular courses, while yet in others, they may be incorporated into one or more training scenarios.

At times, the entire LAPD should receive selected items of information. Lessons might need to be distributed and put to work immediately rather than through the training process. This is especially true for subjects in which refresher training occurs infrequently or for those with immediate impact, such as a potential counterterrorism technique. Alternatively, lessons might go only to supervisors or particular leaders.

The last group of users for LAPD lessons learned—outside police agencies—might at first seem unnecessary. Several of these departments, however, will be neighbors with whom the LAPD consistently interacts in the field: the Los Angeles Sheriff's Office, other Southern California departments, or authorities with overlapping geographic and functional responsibilities (e.g., the FBI). As these various authorities might well work together, sharing lessons learned has potential positive repercussions for officers in all departments involved as well as for the people of Los Angeles. Similar cooperation with more-remote departments, such as those in New York City or Miami, may not yield such immediate benefits. However, reciprocity will eventually benefit policing work more generally and enable the LAPD to fulfill its obligation as a professional force to strengthen American (and perhaps international) law enforcement as a whole.

The Sources of Lessons Learned. A relevant lesson learned can come from virtually any source, such as

- officers in the field

- instructors

- other police departments, professional publications, or events such as conferences

- best practices from other city service agencies

- findings during internal affairs or other investigations

- studies by outside agencies

- sources from those in fields with whom officers routinely work (e.g., fire, military, and emergency medical personnel).

Identifying *who* can provide the stuff of lessons learned is far more straightforward than determining *how* a department taps these potentially rich resources to the benefit of its members and clients.

Getting Lessons to the Field

The complete process of implementing lessons learned requires identifying, collecting, processing, screening, and disseminating them.

Lessons-Learned Collection As a Department-Wide Responsibility. CALL offers valuable approaches for developing and running a lessons-learned program. The center might rely on its internal observers for some of its material, but a considerable amount comes directly from the field. Instructors at training facilities, leaders in units on exercise or deployed on operations, and soldiers themselves are among those who can submit their lessons, observations, ideas, or other material through CALL's field representatives or directly to its headquarters. Given that the LAPD cannot afford a large staff dedicated exclusively to the acquisition of lessons learned, it may wish to implement the more economical procedures CALL uses to obtain insights from the field, those in which soldiers submit input directly to CALL headquarters.

An economical and effective means of collecting such information is the Internet. For the modest cost of establishing supporting web pages, an organization can provide its members with a direct and (if desired) anonymous means of communicating. Suggestion boxes are no longer efficient.

Supporting Recommendation

Encourage but do not pressure contributors to provide contact information. Remember that the receipt of quality lessons learned is the primary goal.

CALL uses the Internet (*http://call.army.mil*) to solicit lessons learned from the U.S. Army's half a million soldiers worldwide. Providing soldiers with an opportunity to answer the question, "How can I Help?" it encourages readers to

> turn those "Ranger Stories" into helpful Lessons Learned, TTPs [tactics, techniques, and procedures], tips and "tools of the trade." Share your training and operational experiences with your peers, Army leaders, Soldiers, and NCOs [non-commissioned officers, i.e.,

corporals and sergeants] throughout the Army. Click <u>HERE</u> to get started.

Clicking on the link immediately takes the user to a form (*http://call.army.mil/forms/call/obser.htm*) for collecting the necessary information in a standard format and allowing him to provide observations and prospective lessons learned. CALL recognizes that the individual inputting the information is, for the purposes of the issue at hand, to be considered the subject matter expert. No one knows more about an idea than the individual proposing it. CALL therefore attempts to recognize that status overtly and treat the contributor in a manner that capitalizes on his willingness to help. The individual is asked to fully explain his contribution, provide what he believes are the pertinent lessons of value, and articulate how the army can best make use of them. Submissions can be anonymous or an individual can choose to provide contact information for feedback. (Providing feedback promotes continued participation. Failure to do so can lead to perceptions that input has been ignored. The occasional difficulty in creating a lesson learned from a less than clearly articulated original suggestion provides a further impetus for maintaining contact with contributors. However, CALL is careful not to pressure the submitter for contact information, understanding that the input is the primary objective.)

This process obviously implies that individuals desiring to provide lessons or observations have access to the Internet. LAPD units could provide access to a common-access computer if their officers do not otherwise have a means of going online during day-to-day operations.

A straightforward method of obtaining lessons learned minimizes setup and maintenance costs. In the case of the LAPD, a link from the Departmental internal home page should take an officer to a lessons submittal page similar to that used by CALL but tailored to meet police needs. Guidance to sergeants, watch commanders, and other supervisors would encourage them to suggest that subordinates submit lessons learned and that they do so themselves. Instructors should be encouraged, if not required, to provide insights from class sessions, as should members of internal affairs teams or others performing investigations in the field. Promotion of participation in the lessons-learned program could take the form of public recognition for particularly valuable ideas, perhaps tied to a monetary reward or points toward promotion for officers and financial prizes or certificates for community members. (As part of a community-policing initiative, the Department could provide members of the public with a similar opportunity to submit lessons learned via an external web site. The likelihood for misuse is high, but there is potential value, both in the demonstration of the Department's interest in public input and from legitimate suggestions forwarded in this manner.)

An LAPD lessons-learned program should not limit its input to suggestions from members of the Department or the local community. The same training group representative who screens suggested lessons should be responsible for monitoring other police web sites, professional journals, and additional external sources of potential value to the LAPD. He or a designated representative should attend law enforcement conferences or conventions with the greatest promise for LAPD-relevant insights. Other members of the Department attending outside professional events should be required to submit candidate lessons learned or make observations regarding advances that seem worthy of the Department's tracking. These reports should include contact information for individuals outside the LAPD from whom more information could be acquired if follow-up is desired.

Processing the Input: Screening and Evaluating. As noted above, no single individual can evaluate the viability or usefulness of all incoming suggestions and recommendations. Some suggestions will need to be referred to those with specialized expertise. Suggestions will also need to be screened for their legal, political, or social implications and possible misunderstanding by the public. Selecting an experienced and mature officer (or retired officer) as the lessons-learned manager will ease much of the administrative burden. Most recommendations can be accepted or rejected by the manager without the need to consult others. These can be consolidated and passed to the manager's supervisor for review and release. Those thought to be potentially sensitive or otherwise worthy of more-detailed evaluation can be forwarded to the appropriate Departmental agency for comment. Exceptional issues could be brought before the commander of the training group or considered by others deemed appropriate before their release.

Spreading the Word: Getting the Lessons Out. Whether a lesson learned "makes the cut" depends in part on its pertinence. Pertinence will also influence where and how the product should be disseminated. Such screening decisions will establish to whom lessons will be made available. The decisions regarding "to whom" will then determine the means used to get the word out: email, the web, or other method. The lessons-learned manager should develop and frequently update various distribution lists that allow him to quickly and effectively get his material to those in target audiences. These lists would include a command version, an instructor roll, watch commanders, and sergeants. Dissemination of appropriate lessons learned—whether daily, weekly, or on an as-needed basis—can thereby be completed efficiently and effectively. Other lessons and observations, those of interest but not essential for targeted dissemination, can be posted to an LAPD lessons-learned web page in a manner similar to that employed by CALL. The manager can suggest to Department leaders that exceptional material appear in articles or sidebars in Department or external publications, including local media. Whether the distribution method is active (e.g., sending word via directed emails) or passive (posting on the web page and thus depending on users to access it voluntarily), the key is to make valuable information available so as to enhance the expertise of Department personnel.

Supporting Recommendation

Create standing distribution lists to facilitate timely and efficient distribution of lessons-learned products.

Concluding Thoughts

Bureaucracies sometimes too closely emulate closed-minded cur-
mudgeons: There is never a new idea that they like. Overwhelmed
with internal and external regulations, requirements, specifications,
policies, political dictates, codes, conditions, limitations, and qualifications, they give innovation short shrift. The penalties for maintaining such an attitude are considerable. Young and inexperienced
minds see problems in ways those long within a system do not. Too
often initiatives born of original insight suffer rejection. An innovation is likely to die before reaching those that could act on it. Experienced law enforcement officers grow so used to doing business as
usual that they might not recognize the brilliance of adaptations they
made months, years, or decades ago. Young or old, police officers
can benefit their colleagues by aiding in educating the whole of the
LAPD. They need only a mechanism for forwarding their ideas and
the motivation to do so. Introducing and nurturing a lessons-
learned program offer the potential for considerable payoff from the
expenditure of very limited resources.

TRANSFORMING JOHN DOE INTO AN LAPD
PROFESSIONAL: BUILDING EXCELLENCE INTO THE
POLICE TRAINING FUNCTION

Primary Recommendation

Introduce and maintain consistently high quality throughout every aspect
of LAPD training.

The Backdrop for Training at the LAPD

The mission of the Los Angeles Police Department Training Group is

> to provide the Department and the City of Los Angeles with the
> finest trained law enforcement professionals in the nation . . . . In
> accomplishing this mission, and while recognizing that we have a
> mandate by the Department to develop its people to their greatest
> potential . . . the management is committed to providing the highest

quality, most realistic and technologically advanced training for all of our employees and reserves.[5]

To make specific training recommendations, we first must delineate the administrative and instructional infrastructure supporting the program under consideration. Our review of written course materials, our classroom observations, and comments by those in the training-coordinator and training-group focus groups all pointed to recurrent shortcomings in curriculum design and instructor skills. In addition, these implements of evaluation reflected the need for a Departmental evaluation process to measure training effectiveness. Subsequent reviews of previous external studies revealed that these same two concerns are recurring issues. Since changes to a curriculum are of little value if instructors present the new material ineffectively, we find it imperative to explain basic training principles.

Even though there are recurrent shortcomings in LAPD training, the Department does have exemplary courses and instructors. There are excellent examples of quality in both academy and post-graduation training. It is the inconsistency of curriculum and instructor quality that is the concern.

The findings of this section are drawn largely from analysis of written material reviews and course observations. When we conducted this fieldwork, each member of the team was assigned a topic area [i.e., (1) use of force, search and seizure, and arrest procedures; (2) community policing and diversity awareness; (3) values, ethics, and professionalism; or (4) professional development of training staff]. The assessment instrument served as the evaluation mechanism (see Appendix B). Reviews regarding given subject areas were eventually integrated to form an overall judgment regarding the area of concern and to identify relevant strengths and weaknesses (see Appendix L).

Training the Professional Police Officer

Training is a fundamental part of the police organization. It is a function of learning as well as teaching. Training not only prepares officers for the job, it also serves as a laboratory where we can think

---

[5]"LAPD Training Group Mission Statement," provided to RAND in November 2002.

deeply about the meaning and essence of policing in a democratic society. By promoting open-minded and leading-edge thinking, the police training contributes to the evolution of the police role in creating a free, diverse, and democratic society for all.

George Gascón
Commander, Training Group, LAPD
June 2001

Educational theorist Jerome Bruner suggests that a curriculum ought to be built around the great issues, principles, and values that society deems worthy of continual concern.[6] Bruner wrote about public education, but his vision is no less applicable to the education of those who serve the public. It is on such a foundation that the Department should construct its curriculum. Success will require that the tenets of professionalism influence both the content of that curriculum and the manner in which it is taught.

The goal of such training is *transformative* learning. Education author Benjamin Bloom describes the lowest levels of learning as rote memory and translation. These are based on information recall and seek simply to transmit information from instructor to student. Intermediate levels of learning include interpretation, application, and analysis, relying on *transaction*—or the ability of students to use logic to discover relationships, solve problems, and reflect on integral parts of the learning processes.[7] The highest levels of learning are synthesis and evaluation. Here the student undergoes *transformative* learning, combining various knowledge, facts, skills, and logic to make unique personal judgments.

Current LAPD recruit training is based on a mid-20th-century military model. Like basic combat training, it seeks to tear down recruits and reconstruct them as LAPD officers. While this is certainly a transformation, the methods employed are more akin to information transmission than transformative learning. Yet the ultimate goal of academy training is to produce a graduate similar to the product of a transformative educational process—an individual skilled in synthe-

---

[6]Rippa, 1969, p. 490.

[7]Glickman, Gordon, and Ross-Gordon, 1995, p. 372.

sis and evaluation and in making informed personal judgments. There may be better ways of developing such an end product than emulating military basic training.

Supporting Recommendation

Clearly articulate the type of officer the Department wants to develop, and use police training to model the behaviors expected of police personnel.

Achieving the desired level of training sophistication (transformative learning) while also screening police candidates and replicating stresses like those found on the streets pose considerable challenges for those running the academy. They have little time and much to accomplish with every recruit. Instructors must establish the sense of unity so important to the concept of corporateness while instilling a sense of responsibility for students to monitor themselves and others. This acculturation process begins on the first day of academy instruction. Trainers teach not only hard skills, they communicate much regarding the expectations of the police profession, the Los Angeles Police Department, and law enforcement leaders. The academy experience should be tailored to ensure that the graduate fully understands expectations for LAPD officers.

Senior police and civilian leadership share a vision of the model LAPD officer as one who has the highest level of integrity, excellent interpersonal and communication skills, and strong problem-solving and decisionmaking ability.[8] All police training—from the first day of the academy through in-service, supervisor, manager, and command-development instruction—must work toward the goal of developing this type of officer. Classroom observations, focus groups with trainees and trainers, and community and LAPD interviews all indicate that current training does not achieve this. During one classroom observation period, the instructors themselves were at odds over how to handle chain-of-command reporting, officer ethics, and safety issues. Many LAPD members could not identify what the

[8]James K. Hahn, Mayor, City of Los Angeles, interview by Estela Lopez and Barbara R. Panitch, December 5, 2002; LAPD Chief of Police William J. Bratton, interview by Russell Glenn and Barbara R. Panitch, February 13, 2003.

Department specifically expected of its officers when the question was posed during interviews and focus group sessions. Those who did respond contradicted each other, suggesting that whatever training is being offered in this regard is ineffective.

Educational Techniques

Effective training demands appropriate educational techniques. The traditional discipline-based classroom training environment currently employed during much of academy instruction may limit student learning.

Adult learners need a form of education that recognizes their higher cognitive development, existing knowledge base, and extensive life experiences.[9]

Experts advise that adult education should incorporate six learning principles:[10]

- Adults learn throughout their lives.

- They exhibit diverse learning styles and learn in different ways, at different times, for different purposes.

- As a rule, they like their learning activities to be problem centered and to be meaningful to their life situation.

- Adults want their learning outcomes to have some immediacy of application.

- The past experiences of adults affect their current learning, sometimes serving as an enhancement, sometimes a hindrance.

- Adults exhibit a tendency toward self-directedness in their learning.

---

[9]LAPD, 2001.

[10]Haney, 1998.

Supporting Recommendation

Employ theoretically grounded adult educational techniques such as interactive methods and self-directed learning.

Classroom observations indicate that the LAPD's in-service curriculum is more reflective of such principles than is current Department recruit training. While academy staff are seeking to bring their curriculum into line with accepted adult learning practices, it remains tied to more traditional classroom models in those sessions we viewed. Table 3.1 reflects this dichotomy.

Changing training methods from a military basic training model to one emphasizing adult learning would by no means imply that recruits should not be rigorously tested. Academy training that does not adequately screen its students would fail to act as an appropriate

Table 3.1

**Training Methods Employed During LAPD
Recruit Instruction**

Training Method	Percentage of all LAPD Courses
Adult learning	75%
Traditional	82%
Technical	25%
Multimedia	53%
Other	32%

NOTES: One or more of each type of method was found to be used (as part of each percentage shown):

- Adult learning: Case study/scenario, facilitation, learning activity, problem based (begin session with researching a problem), role playing, self-paced, simulator training, table top (simulation/vignette).
- Traditional: Anecdotes/examples given, lecture, questions and answers, workbook.
- Technical: Demonstration; repetitive drill.
- Multimedia: PowerPoint presentation as outline, PowerPoint file that is interactive.
- Other: Use of student questioning, explicit checks for understanding.

prerequisite for entry into the law enforcement profession. Demanding standards must be established and maintained. Situations that replicate the stress an officer is likely to confront must remain part of the training curriculum. Designing such training is far more difficult than introducing stress in the traditional basic training style. It will require innovation, adaptation, frequent updating, and an effective approach.

Problem-based learning is one means of meeting both the objectives of transformative learning and adequately testing/screening recruits. It employs an experiential activity-based format designed to take advantage of an adult learner's level of cognitive development.

Problem-based learning places students in the active role of problem solvers who are confronted with complex problems similar to those confronted in workplace situations. The model is learner centered and facilitates the transfer of knowledge from a classroom environment to real-life settings. Properly conducted, problem-based learning promotes collaboration, builds teamwork skills, and develops leadership abilities through cooperative work-group experiences. Students move through a series of inquiries involving the generation of ideas and discussion of known facts and learning issues. Participants then develop a plan of action to resolve problems and evaluate the learning process. Many medical schools, law schools, and business schools have adopted problem-based learning in recent years.

The process itself causes students to work as a team while the instructor serves as facilitator. Team members identify and prioritize relevant issues using a four-step method similar to the community policing SARA model (scanning, analysis, response, and assessment; Chapter Four includes a more detailed discussion of the SARA problem-solving process). Students are encouraged to supplement the curriculum with personal knowledge, experiences, and additional classroom research. Their shared task is not only to learn the material under consideration, but also to become increasingly capable of directing their own training activities and education.

Problem-based learning is increasingly being employed as a particularly appropriate model for police students. Law enforcement agencies across the country are implementing problem-based learning in their recruit, field, and in-service training. The Royal Canadian Mounted Police force has designed its recruit training in accordance with this model's dictates. The Reno, Nevada, police department; that in Charlotte-Mecklenburg, North Carolina; and five other agencies are piloting a field training model that grounds both the instruction for field trainers and field training itself in a problem-based model.

Curriculum Design

Competent curriculum design is essential to training excellence. Determining the instruction's purpose, content, organization, and format establishes the basis for good curriculum design.[11] Below we address each of these four elements in turn.

What should the *purpose* of a curriculum be?

The goal or purpose of much professional education is to develop responsive personnel with appropriate technical skills who can make correct decisions on their own.[12] This means that the LAPD Training Group should combine instruction regarding the many specific elements of police expertise with those that address an ability to adapt to expected and unexpected situations in the work environment.

What should the instruction *content* be?

Every profession has a set of skills that are unique to it. (The expertise unique to the police profession receives greater attention in Chapter Five.) Competency-based learning addresses the dual requirements of an officer needing both a basic skill set and the ability to adapt to situations effectively. It entails instruction in which officers develop selected skills that are general in nature and transferable to many situations.[13]

---

[11]Glickman, Gordon, and Ross-Gordon, 1995, p. 354.

[12]Ibid.

[13]Joan Sweeney, educational consultant, interview by Barbara R. Panitch and Dionne Barnes, February 17, 2003.

Supporting Recommendation

Maintain consistent and high-quality curriculum design and instructor performance throughout the Department.

How should the Department *organize* its curriculum?

There are three broad approaches to organizing curriculum content: discipline based, interdisciplinary, and transdisciplinary. Discipline-based curricula present information in discrete segments with each subject having a separate time block. There is no attempt to show relationships among them. This method suits basic information *transmission*, or rote learning.[14]

In an interdisciplinary curriculum, common themes connect traditional content areas. For policing, this could mean that community policing and diversity awareness are combined to form an instructional theme. Students are encouraged to discover relationships and develop applications across existing content areas through what is known as *transaction* learning.

The third approach to organizing a curriculum is transdisciplinary. In this case, an entire curriculum is organized around common themes, skills, or problems. Students do much of their learning through self-discovery and group interaction. Transdisciplinary curricula seek *transformative* learning. Problem-based learning is typically transdisciplinary.

A combination of these organizational methods will likely be most appropriate for police training. Technical skills, such as handling a weapon, provide a good example of where clear and concise transmission of information is critical. There is little need or desire for individual variation in weapon use. There is, however, a good deal of demand for individual decisionmaking and judgment during use-of-force or arrest-procedure instruction. An officer must be able to both execute specific drills and apply sound judgment during what can be very different situations. He is more likely to develop the ability to

---

[14]Glickman, Gordon, and Ross-Gordon, 1995, p. 375.

simultaneously exercise these many abilities through a curriculum that encourages transformative learning.

What should the *format* be?

The LAPD should use a standardized format for course outlines, lesson plans, and other written curriculum materials. The training group should develop a program for creating or revising all appropriate LAPD course materials, including individual lesson plans. The program should include a schedule for creating or revising all Department lesson plans. All work within the confines of this program should be completed by March 31, 2006.

Supporting Recommendation

Develop uniform format guidelines for written curriculum materials and revise instructional materials to meet those guidelines. Complete Department-wide revisions no later than March 31, 2006.

Any standardized format should include

- name of course or lesson
- overall goal and specific objectives of course or lesson
- a list of the core values of the Department and where they are emphasized in the curriculum
- discussion of how areas of particular emphasis (e.g., community policing, diversity awareness, interactive scenarios, and problem solving) are integrated into the instructional materials
- specific knowledge expected of students at completion of the course or lesson.

The LAPD initiated the standardization of its written curricula prior to the commencement of this research.[15] While the existing guid-

---

[15]Sergio Diaz, Captain, Training Division, interview by Russell Glenn and Barbara R. Panitch, August 29, 2002; Mark Olvera, Lieutenant, Training Division, interview by Dionne Barnes, August 29, 2002; Robin Greene, Director of Training and Education, interview by Barbara R. Panitch, February 10, 2003.

ance may require revision in light of changes resulting from this study, this Department initiative is a positive initial step. Standardizing the written format will make it easier for course evaluations to track the congruence of written lesson plans and course material as actually taught during class sessions. Standardization will also assist in efforts to validate that the instruction as designed meets Department and training group objectives.

Models of Teaching—Instructor Development and Delivery

Development of high-quality curricula is a vital first step. The next is ensuring that capable instructors present the materials. Law enforcement personnel are rarely hired for their teaching skills. As staff at the FBI academy found, instructors need to be taught how to educate effectively.[16] The current quality of instructor training in the LAPD falls well short of acceptable standards.

Current LAPD instruction ranges from excellent to unacceptable. It is particularly critical that those in such positions as instructor development and field-training-officer (FTO) development are effective teachers and capable of developing quality faculty.

Unfortunately, the training group lacks sufficient authority to set and maintain uniform standards for LAPD instructors. This problem is due to a combination of factors, including lack of selection authority for many officers in teaching positions (e.g., FTOs), Department personnel policies, union or other external bureaucratic influences, and a division of instructor oversight responsibility within the training group itself. The Los Angeles Police Department should centralize the authority to set teaching standards, conduct instructor training, and validate instructors before they are allowed to train others. This centralization of authority should include the power to remove instructors who fail to perform acceptably.

---

[16]FBI trainers' interview by Russell Glenn, July 23, 2002.

Supporting Recommendation

Vest the training group with the power to validate instructors before they are allowed to train others and to remove instructors who fail to maintain acceptable levels of training performance.

The instructor development course (IDC) requires revamping both on paper and in practice if it is to come into line with the adult learning principles and the scenario training that the Department is already appropriately advancing as its preferred instructional technique. Every LAPD instructor should have to successfully complete a revised and better taught IDC. Such a course would train candidate instructors and test their ability to prepare educational materials, train effectively, facilitate group learning, and otherwise orchestrate classroom activities. Instructor evaluation should additionally include validation of an individual's subject matter expertise in the areas for which he is responsible. After a Departmental transition period, no individual should be allowed to train LAPD personnel prior to successful IDC completion. Exceptions can be made for guest instructors from outside the LAPD, but the training group should audit these individuals' classes and bar those whose performance does not meet established standards. When possible, individuals wishing to invite outside instructors should observe them beforehand to assure the quality of instruction.

Supporting Recommendation

Do not allow any LAPD instructor to train officers prior to his successful completion of the Department instructor development course.

Successful teaching requires practice. An instructor needs to be familiar with his material and comfortable teaching it. Repeated practice with a variety of audiences, including peers and master instructors, is necessary for honing teaching skills and achieving classroom success. Practice audiences should provide constructive evaluations of instructor performance.[17]

Establishment of high standards and rigorous testing does not imply that those educating LAPD officers will be automatons. It would be counterproductive were every class to follow an identical format and employ the same training aids. Instructors must have a great deal of discretion in selecting a teaching style and in choosing the means they use to communicate with their students. They will operate with relatively little surveillance and few standard operating procedures, which will have a number of implications. Instructor standards for the LAPD must be clearly articulated and followed. The concept of professionalism applies here no less than elsewhere. Department members have a duty to ensure that trainers meet established standards (corporate self-policing) and possess the mastery of techniques and material (expertise) needed to properly prepare others to serve society (responsibility).

We are not implying that drills and repetition do not have a role in law enforcement training. As mentioned above, it is likely that the LAPD will appropriately choose to continue to develop basic tactical and technical expertise through its current methods of training (those favoring rote memorization and transmission of procedural facts).

Instructors who have previously employed the use of lectures and other traditional "direct" instruction formats will find adoption of problem-based learning a challenge. Sending proven instructors to the Royal Canadian Mounted Police department training, the FBI academy, or other institutions familiar with performance-based learning may help instructors make the transition. It is essential that these unfamiliar approaches be well understood. It is therefore criti-

---

[17]Diaz interview, 2002.

cal that instructor candidates receive training from and observe teaching by others experienced in problem-based learning. This initial training must include extensive practice in applying this technique in the presence of veterans in its use.

Most instructor candidates will be unaccustomed to engaging in the problem-solving activities that characterize problem-based learning. Those providing instructor training will need to guide their instructor recruits through such exercises to build their confidence in the approach. If the instructor is open with his students, as those teaching problem-based learning should be, then students will learn not only via the material presented but also by example of those they are observing.

The Case for Evaluating Training Programs

The final step of the training development process is evaluation. The limited time frame allotted to our project did not allow sufficient time for the LAPD to implement recommended changes and for us to then measure the results. Nevertheless, we acknowledge and stress the importance of thoroughly and regularly evaluating training effectiveness. Improving training is a continual process involving a cycle of instruction, evaluation, and adjustment.

It is not enough to test learning when a student completes a course. Evaluation should also focus on performance in the field. Recognizing this, the LAPD has initiated work toward a "results-based" evaluation model.[18] Introduction of a lessons-learned-feedback mechanism will offer further means for evaluation of training; former students should be encouraged to provide their observations on the strengths and weaknesses of the training they have received, the objective being adjustment of that training to meet field requirements.

Many organizations do little to measure training effectiveness.[19] Field evaluation can be expensive and disruptive. Managers forgo evaluation because training often addresses competencies that do not easily lend themselves to quantified measurement. Training

---

[18]Murphy and Gascón, 2001, p. 3.

[19]Jenkins, 2002, p. 3.

evaluations are therefore frequently limited to "smile sheets," the course evaluation forms that trainees complete at the end of instruction. Formal measurement beyond this type of evaluation sheet is rare. Experts in training and development agree that these are not valid excuses for failing to evaluate training effectiveness.[20]

The RAND assessment instrument (see Appendix B) used in support of data collection for this study can be used to assist the LAPD in conducting evaluations to gauge the effectiveness of its training. Whether used by training group evaluators, Department leaders designated to observe training, or other personnel, the instrument provides a starting point for use in both evaluating written material and making classroom observations. It should be noted that while there certainly should be correlation between what is taught to recruits and officers and how they later perform in the field, there are many confounding variables (i.e., influences other than training) that also affect that performance. Thus any evaluation of performance needs to consider the influence of training and of these other factors that have positive or negative effects on performance in the field.

LAPD Approach to Training Evaluation. The LAPD has embarked on a centralized training delivery approach for post-academy officer education. This approach, the Continuing Education Delivery Plan (CEDP), includes a corresponding training evaluation process. The CEDP design team chose to implement an evaluation mechanism that consists of multilevel analysis of training outcomes.[21] This model is sometimes called the four-level model or the Kirkpatrick model after the name of its proponent, Donald L. Kirkpatrick.[22] The four levels are the parameters to be evaluated: reaction, learning, behavior, and results.

Reaction refers to participants' responses to the training program. It is a measure of participant satisfaction with training.[23] At its most basic level, reaction is measured using course evaluation forms. This is a relatively simple parameter to measure that is commonly tracked

---

[20]Kirkpatrick, 1998, p. xv.

[21]Murphy and Gascón, 2001, p. 3.

[22]Kirkpatrick, 1998, p. xv.

[23]Ibid., p. 25.

by organizations. The LAPD has addressed this first level by designing course critiques to gauge officers' opinions of training.[24]

The second evaluation level, learning, encompasses the knowledge, skills, and/or attitudes affected or improved by training. Measuring learning involves gauging the extent to which trainees absorbed the content of what was taught. Kirkpatrick proposes that one or more of the following questions should be answered: What knowledge was learned? What skills were developed or improved? What attitudes were changed? The LAPD designed assessment tools to survey comprehension and retention of training topics to meet this demand.[25]

Behavior, the third evaluation level, refers to training's effect on individual behavior. Training is not conducted simply for education and retention sake; improvement of individuals' performance in the field is critical. Behavior is more difficult to measure than learning, but Kirkpatrick suggests methodologies such as testing before and after training and comparing the results with those of a control group where practical. The major difference between testing involving level two (learning) and level three (behavior) is that in the latter case the evaluation is conducted through people who work with the trainee—supervisors, peers, and/or subordinates—rather than the trainee himself. Surveys of and focus groups with police officers and community members are the tools the LAPD plans to employ to track behavior change.[26]

The fourth and final training evaluation level, results, is concerned with the tangible outcomes of training. These generally refer to attainment of organizational as opposed to individual goals. All organizations ultimately expect to see "bottom-line" results from training. Results, however, are difficult to measure. The primary caveat regarding evaluation at level four is that the results should not be expected to unequivocally reflect the actual value of a training program. Results-based evaluation can reveal evidence that training has succeeded in achieving organizational goals, but it is rarely if ever possible to establish a causative relationship when the goals are top-

---

[24]Murphy and Gascón, 2001, p. 3.

[25]Ibid.

[26]Murphy and Gascón, 2001, p. 3.

level measures influenced by many different factors. In general, results-based evaluation works best when the training is aimed at specific, quantifiable organizational objectives that can be easily measured and that have a strong causal relationship with the techniques or skills being trained. The LAPD intends to address this evaluation level by conducting return-on-investment (ROI) analyses of training programs.[27] The ROI analysis will compare training costs with risk management costs such as lawsuits and awards against the Department.

The LAPD has reported some preliminary results of CEDP evaluation involving levels one and two of the four-level model: reaction and learning. The Department has not yet attempted level three and four evaluations. The LAPD has used these early results to establish a knowledge baseline and direct remedial training. It had not employed the results of its training evaluation to alter curriculum, delivery, or other aspects of training or workforce management at the time of this writing.[28]

Supporting Recommendation

Implement procedures to use all four levels of the Kirkpatrick model to evaluate Department training effectiveness.

There are evaluation models that compete with the Kirkpatrick approach. There seems to be no reason to change course at this time given that the Department has already adopted and is employing the four-level method and given the relative ease and low cost of its use compared with most alternatives. LAPD valuation objectives can be achieved through the use of this model if it is applied with all four levels incorporated.

---

[27]Ibid.

[28]Greene interview, 2003; Captain William Sutton (continuing education division, CED) and Lieutenant William Murphy (CED), interview by Barbara R. Panitch, February 3, 2003; Murphy and Gascón, 2001.

The relevance of training evaluation to professionalism is clear. Evaluation provides a self-policing means of measuring instructor effectiveness and officer expertise.

CURRENT LAPD TRAINING ORGANIZATION STRUCTURE

The purpose of the following section is to give a brief overview of the current organization of the LAPD's training function (see Figure 3.1) and how structure relates to some of our findings regarding police training.

The LAPD Training Group is currently commanded by the Chief of Support Services, who reports directly to the Office of the Chief of Police. The Assistant Chief in charge of Human Resources directly supervises four positions, one of which is the commander who heads the training group. Within the training group there are three major functional areas: the training division, the continuing education division (CED), and police training and education.

The training division has primary responsibility for recruit training. The commanding officer (CO) fills a captain-level position and in turn has responsibility for three subordinate groups: the Davis training facility section, the recruit training section, and the administrative training section. Each of these groups has several functional training units. For example, the recruit training section includes academic instruction, physical fitness/self defense, Spanish, legal, and human relations training units. There are a total of 195 staff positions in the training division, including 154 sworn officers and 41 civilians.[29]

The CED is primarily responsible for in-service training to experienced officers. Like the training division, the commanding officer occupies a captain-level position with three reporting functional areas. These are the training and support section, the professional development section, and the research and development section. Each section is divided further into smaller units; for example, the training

---

[29]LAPD data as of March 2003. Numbers include vacant positions and pending changes proposed at the LAPD Staff Officers' Annual Retreat (SOAR), Oxnard, Calif., January 26, 2003.

Current LAPD Training Organization Structure

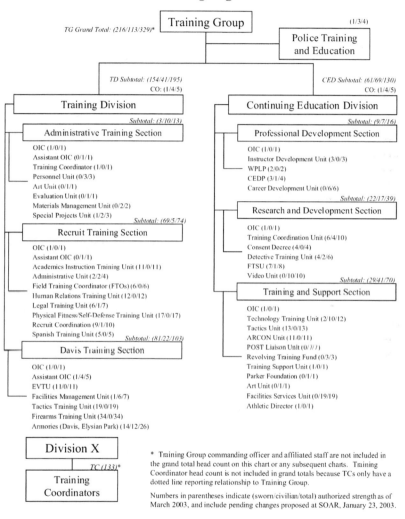

Training Group

TG Grand Total: (216/113/329)*

(1/3/4)

Police Training and Education

TD Subtotal: (154/41/195)
CO: (1/4/5)

CED Subtotal: (61/69/130)
CO: (1/4/5)

Training Division

Subtotal: (3/10/13)

Administrative Training Section

OIC (1/0/1)
Assistant OIC (0/1/1)
Training Coordinator (1/0/1)
Personnel Unit (0/3/3)
Art Unit (0/1/1)
Evaluation Unit (0/1/1)
Materials Management Unit (0/2/2)
Special Projects Unit (1/2/3)

Subtotal: (69/5/74)

Recruit Training Section

OIC (1/0/1)
Assistant OIC (0/1/1)
Academics Instruction Training Unit (11/0/11)
Administrative Unit (2/2/4)
Field Training Coordinator (FTOs) (6/0/6)
Human Relations Training Unit (12/0/12)
Legal Training Unit (6/1/7)
Physical Fitness/Self-Defense Training Unit (17/0/17)
Recruit Coordination (9/1/10)
Spanish Training Unit (5/0/5)

Subtotal: (81/22/103)

Davis Training Section

OIC (1/0/1)
Assistant OIC (1/4/5)
EVTU (11/0/11)
Facilities Management Unit (1/6/7)
Tactics Training Unit (19/0/19)
Firearms Training Unit (34/0/34)
Armories (Davis, Elysian Park) (14/12/26)

Continuing Education Division

Subtotal: (9/7/16)

Professional Development Section

OIC (1/0/1)
Instructor Development Unit (3/0/3)
WPLP (2/0/2)
CEDP (3/1/4)
Career Development Unit (0/6/6)

Subtotal: (22/17/39)

Research and Development Section

OIC (1/0/1)
Training Coordination Unit (6/4/10)
Consent Decree (4/0/4)
Detective Training Unit (4/2/6)
FTSU (7/1/8)
Video Unit (0/10/10)

Subtotal: (29/41/70)

Training and Support Section

OIC (1/0/1)
Technology Training Unit (2/10/12)
Tactics Unit (13/0/13)
ARCON Unit (11/0/11)
POST Liaison Unit (0/1/1)
Revolving Training Fund (0/3/3)
Training Support Unit (1/0/1)
Parker Foundation (0/1/1)
Art Unit (0/1/1)
Facilities Services Unit (0/19/19)
Athletic Director (1/0/1)

Division X

TC (133)*

Training Coordinators

* Training Group commanding officer and affiliated staff are not included in the grand total head count on this chart or any subsequent charts. Training Coordinator head count is not included in grand totals because TCs only have a dotted line reporting relationship to Training Group.

Numbers in parentheses indicate (sworn/civilian/total) authorized strength as of March 2003, and include pending changes proposed at SOAR, January 23, 2003.

SOURCE: Robin Greene, Director of Training and Education, interview by Barbara R. Panitch, February 10, 2003.

Figure 3.1

and support section has a tactics unit, an arrest and control (ARCON) unit, POST liaison unit, and others. There are 130 total personnel in the CED, including 61 sworn officers and 69 civilians.[30]

The police training and education group is small, including an authorized strength of three civilians and one sworn officer. Its primary mission is to provide subject matter expertise in the area of adult learning and to review and evaluate training policies, curricula, and program delivery for the LAPD. A director-level position heads the group. Notably, while it has the *responsibility* to oversee these areas, it lacks the *authority* to set standards and enforce them.

There are several other training functions distributed throughout the Department that do not fall directly under any one of these three training group core training components. The foremost of these is the FTO role that serves as the principal on-the-job training resource for probationary officers. Similar to other police departments, the program pairs a rookie officer (probationer) with an FTO, whose job is to provide training, supervision, and evaluation during the less experienced officer's transition from academy to patrol. There are roughly 900 FTOs in the LAPD. Training coordinators are another such training resource. A training coordinator is a sworn officer located in a bureau or division who provides various training-related services. These include myriad administrative training activities such as conducting training needs assessment for his organization's personnel, scheduling training programs, and performing ancillary duties such as reviewing use-of-force cases. Many training coordinators also serve part-time as instructors for CEDP training. There are 133 training coordinators in the LAPD at the given time.[31] The full-time position of training coordinator developed out of a desire to provide locally focused training programs and training activities; it represented an effort to provide local, decentralized training services in an otherwise centralized model.[32] It is worth noting that training coordinators technically have no reporting relationship to the training group even though they serve part-time as instructors there. The

---

[30]Ibid.

[31]LAPD training coordinator roster, November 2002.

[32]"A Training Analysis of the Los Angeles Police Department," October 21, 1991.

training group does not have control over their selection or retention.[33]

There are several other training functions embedded within the LAPD that notionally report to the CED but are virtually autonomous. For example, there are training resources devoted to investigative analysis training, juvenile school, and information technology training. These functions represent a way of providing subject-matter-specific learning and development programs.

There are proposed training organization structure changes pending at the LAPD at the time of this writing. LAPD leadership discussed reallocation of some decentralized training resources during the January 2003 LAPD Staff Officers' Annual Retreat (SOAR). Among the suggested changes were to

*   move oversight of FTO training to the training division

*   move career development, detective/investigative analysis training, and technical (information technology) training to the CED.[34]

The ultimate disposition of these proposals is pending.

Together these training elements combine to form the vehicle of instruction for the LAPD's sworn and civilian personnel.

GUIDING PRINCIPLES FOR THE RESTRUCTURING OF THE TRAINING GROUP

Primary Recommendation

Restructure the LAPD Training Group to allow the centralization of planning; instructor qualification, evaluation, and learning retention; and more efficient use of resources.

---

[33]Assistant Chief George Gascón, LAPD, interview by Russell Glenn and Barbara R. Panitch, December 10, 2002.

[34]LAPD SOAR conference, Oxnard, Calif., January 26, 2003; LAPD proposed organization charts (see later in this chapter).

The rationale for changing the organizational structure of the LAPD training function derives from two guiding principles set out in this book. The first of these is the ethic of police professionalism. The second is the proposed shift away from compartmentalized training toward a more integrated approach that ensures continuity among recruit, continuing education, and all other instruction. These guiding principles should underpin all decisions the LAPD makes regarding its training organization structure.

A key implication of the requirement for adherence to standards that the concept of corporateness implies is the need to centralize the responsibility and authority for training curriculum development, delivery, and assessment. Centralization implies that a single authority has the job of ensuring that Department-wide training is being conducted in accordance with professional standards. The central authority must have oversight of all instructors to ensure the consistency, clarity, and quality of the messages being delivered to all recruits and officers. The central authority must also administer formal performance management processes for instructors and others directly involved in training to maintain management accountability and improve the quality of the training function.

The reorganization ramifications of less compartmentalized, more integrated instruction are significant ones. The nature of the work performed by an organization should in general drive its organization structure. If the LAPD fundamentally changes the way it trains its officers by ensuring continuity throughout its curriculum as this book proposes, it should restructure its training organization to reflect the new way of doing business. It is irrational to make fundamental changes to the content of training only to leave the organization structure as it currently stands. To use a hypothetical example, assume that there is a company that has separate organizations for sales and customer service. After some analysis, the company determines that it can increase sales and improve customer satisfaction by taking a more integrated approach to the sales and service process. If the company adopts this new work process, it should also consolidate its sales and customer service organizations to reflect the change. Similarly, if the LAPD adopts a less segmented training approach in which some topics are integrated into others (as is also proposed with the integration of community policing and diversity into all aspects of training), then the structure of its educational organization should reflect the change.

How does this guiding principle specifically affect the LAPD? Primarily, it means that the Department will need to develop a cadre of instructors who are well versed in all aspects of the integrated training approach, are not narrowly confined to functional categories, and teach throughout the training system (e.g., recruit training as well as continuing education). Certain technically demanding skills or highly specific knowledge bases may still call for the functional division of responsibilities—for example, specialized instruction in the use of firearms—but a considerable proportion of the faculty should be generalists who have a comprehensive understanding of what it means to be a professional police officer in today's world. (It should be noted that some classes could combine these two groups, matching the generalist who is predominantly responsible for conducting a session with a specialist who assists with a technical subject area.) An organization composed of generalist instructors who teach via an integrated training approach needs to have a centralized resource responsible for oversight. This is a consequence of the corporate element of professionalism: Self-policing and regulation of standards are paramount. Otherwise, training standards are likely to degenerate naturally over time as distinct cells of training experts exert influence over content and methods and nonexperts supervise instruction. Again, it bears repeating that some degree of divergence in training based on context-specific differences is inevitable and even desirable; however, the Department's training organization needs an ultimate arbiter to determine how and when training can deviate from Department standards.

The ability to share training resources among recruit training, continuing education, and other functions is key to Department-wide consistency in subject matter coverage as well as standards of instructor performance. As it exists now, the LAPD Training Group has separate functional divisions for recruit and in-service training. By better consolidating instructional resources between the two functions, the LAPD could abet both this consistency and a reduction in the training resources needed to teach similar subject matter to different audiences. The first of these benefits is straightforward. If the same instructor teaches both novice officers and those with experience in the field, there will be less variance in the institutional knowledge imparted to each group. There should also be a more effective hierarchy of instructional presentation; i.e., what is taught to officers in the field should build on and complement, not simply repeat, what recruits receive. Overly similar training to both groups can be avoided as training oversight and instructors deliberately design progressive classes. Jarring gaps between functional area material should likewise be avoidable.

The second benefit (reduction of training resources) is less obvious. It presumes that there are redundancies in resources; for example, two instructors teach the same subject matter to different groups of trainees. If this is true, then consolidating the instructor corps would free staff resources—for example, effective centralized scheduling should, in some cases, permit a single trainer to handle the burden currently borne by two. Of course, the instructor-trainee dynamic is somewhat different from that for recruits and for those receiving in-service training.[35] There is no reason this difference has to be an insurmountable obstacle if instructor quality achieves desirable levels via changes as previously discussed.

Supporting Recommendation

Carefully plan and implement restructuring to minimize organizational and personal turbulence.

So far the motivation for restructuring LAPD training has been discussed in terms of two guiding principles: the corporateness element of police professionalism and an integrated training approach. Both of these reflect the desire of the LAPD to improve training quality as part of its ongoing efforts to improve service to the community. There are two additional, supporting considerations that should direct the LAPD's decisions regarding restructuring. First, personnel reductions in training are a likely outcome of restructuring and should be factored into the analysis. As mentioned above, there are likely to be synergies that arise from the consolidation and centralization of certain training activities. For instance, in addition to re-

---

[35]Sutton and Murphy interview, 2003; training coordinator focus group notes, November 14, 2002.

ducing numbers by taking advantage of instructors teaching the same material to different audiences, scheduling could be handled in a more centralized manner, obviating the need for multiple staff members to perform the work in separate units. Second, the Department should seek to minimize organizational disruptions to the greatest extent possible as it pursues structural changes. The recommendations for organization structure by no means require a complete dismantling of the structure as it currently exists. The LAPD should capitalize on continuities (e.g., by assigning individuals to positions that best take advantage of their experience and demonstrated talents) and program its implementation to allow continuity in functions rather than closing down aspects of training for extended periods. Such a plan might include the following steps:

- Gather data and complete reorganization analyses.

- Share proposed organization design(s) with key stakeholders.

- Finalize redesign and communicate the changes to those affected.

- Set the timetable for changes to reporting relationships and addition, elimination, or physical movement of positions, perhaps taking advantage of training schedule slack time and heavy vacation periods (during which individuals' offices could be moved for them).

- Carry out changes and assess progress.

The time required to conduct the reorganization should be determined less by haste and more by efficiency and minimization of organizational and personnel disruptions. It could conceivably be completed in three to four months. It should be possible to complete without undue difficulty within a year. The major variable is whether the LAPD automates its training management system and the accompanying training time that is deemed necessary to support that automation. In addition to affecting the transition schedule, automation would significantly influence the character of the final training group structure. Restructuring should occur simultaneously with any move to greater automation; personnel intimately involved with automated processes would require training before their positions could be considered fully functional.

Supporting Recommendation

Carefully coordinate reorganization with any further automation of training group functions.

TRAINING ORGANIZATION STRUCTURE FINDINGS

RAND analysis in support of this book identified several ways in which the LAPD's training organization structure does not conform to the demands of a training paradigm that emphasizes police professionalism and integrated training. In particular, the corporate requirements of enforcing standards and self-policing demand that Department instruction meet acceptable standards. Without high-quality instruction, the LAPD cannot expect its members to gain the level of expertise essential to serving society effectively. The present arrangement of training resources within LAPD supports a training model that is appropriate for building technical proficiency for which the Department was especially known in past decades. Moving ahead, LAPD's training organization requires adjustments that reflect the internal and external forces that are shaping its future role as a servant of the community.

Perhaps the most immediate shortcoming of the current organization structure is its inability to provide adequate continuity between recruit and field training. FTOs suggest that they do not know what is taught in the academy, stating that they have to ask recruits what they learned. (Note: Training group personnel are aware of this issue and have recently housed the FTO program in the academy as a first step to integrating recruit and field training.) Current evidence suggests that LAPD officers sometimes receive very different instruction from the time they start at the academy to the time they receive training in the field as veteran officers. As previously noted, continuing education should not simply repeat what is taught in the academy. However, it is essential that recruit training be consistent with the demands of service in the field. Similarly, continuing education instruction has to be consistent with and support academy training. This will help to address the common refrain that FTOs teach officers to "forget what [they] learned in the academy."[36] Uniformity of training messages is considered a "huge problem."[37] Further evidence of a fissure between recruit and field training came from officers' comments that were centered on the lack of "real-life" training in the academy, which is perceived as less rigorous and challenging than it should be to prepare them for the challenges of the street.[38] Regarding ongoing instruction, comments were also made about CED instruction being out of touch and "ivory tower" in substance.[39] The key flaw implied by these findings from a structural perspective is a lack of coordination and communication between the resources allocated to recruit and in-service training. Philosophically, too, it appears that conflicting values are at play. The FTO reorganization that is under way at the LAPD is critical to complement other structural changes recommended here.

The authority for ensuring that a shared message is delivered in all training venues is diffused over different training functions. Although the authority for ensuring consistent training messages is nominally assigned to the head of the training group, the sizable workload involved prevents all of these vital roles from being performed by one staff member. The result of such an authority vacuum is a progression toward different value systems and away from uniform standards.

Another major finding is that the LAPD Training Group has no real entity in charge of curriculum development and training quality assurance.[40] Apart from the commander-level position that heads the training group—which ostensibly has authority and control over all curriculum development and training delivery decisions—there is no single unit that has the responsibility to perform all of the day-to-day activities associated with these functions within the group. Nor does the training group's commander have control over FTO, training coordinator, or other training functions as identified above. Authority

---

[36]LAPD probationers focus group notes, December 14, 2002.

[37]Gascón interview, 2002.

[38]LAPD FTO focus group notes, December 14, 2002.

[39]Ibid.

[40]Sutton and Murphy interview, 2003; Greene interview, 2003; Gascón interview, 2002.

and workload are diffused throughout the Department. The consequence of this structural arrangement is that there is no unit with the
authority to control a variety of vital training activities, including
oversight of instructor selection, deselection, and training; development and review of major components of the training curriculum;
audit and evaluation of training programs to ensure consistency with
the Department's mission, goals, and values; and restructuring of all
LAPD training. Variants of this finding were cited in past studies. It
remains a key area of opportunity for the LAPD.[41]

In a related matter, the CED has an acute problem with instructor resources. As noted, centralization of training management authority
as recommended here would assign all faculty members into a single
organization—what henceforth will be referred to as the "training
oversight" function. Specifically, the CED borrows training coordinators for CEDP module instruction on a part-time basis. As a result,
the CED does not have the full-time resources it requires to adequately deliver in-service training.[42] The organizational boundaries
between the training division and the CED mean that recruit instructors and continuing education instructors are distinct. This gener-
ates the aforementioned problems of consistency in the delivery of
training messages and inefficient allocation of staff resources. There
are also indications that the Department too rarely makes use of instructor resources, to include non-sworn personnel, from outside the
LAPD.[43]

Another finding related to training organization structure (one discussed at length earlier in this chapter) shows that there are no formal mechanisms for incorporating lessons learned into training. The
LAPD conducts some ad hoc activities to capture knowledge from
the field and other police agencies, but these efforts are largely informal and rarely focus on "softer" areas such as training.[44] The
LAPD does not have training group staff positions with primary re-

---

[41]See "Department Analysis of Rampart Independent Review Panel Recommenda-
tions," January 25, 2003; "A Training Analysis of the Los Angeles Police Department,"
October 21, 1991; and "In the Course of Change: The Los Angeles Police Department
Five Years After the Christopher Commission," May 30, 1996.

[42]Sutton and Murphy interview, 2003; Gascón interview, 2002.

[43]Gascón interview, 2002.

[44]Meeting with City of Los Angeles representatives, July 8, 2002.

sponsibility for acquiring and disseminating internal and external lessons learned, nor does it have the processes or information systems to facilitate such information exchange. Training coordinators in the divisions have some degree of responsibility for collecting lessons learned from the field (especially in complaint and use-of-force reviews) and distributing the information to officers in their divisions as a learning device, but this distribution of knowledge is not a comprehensive process.[45] The absence of a mechanism to incorporate lessons learned into training has a variety of consequences. In the most extreme outcomes, failure to learn from errors can lead to serious risk exposure for the Department. More typically, the lack of a structure and/or processes to capture best practices means that the LAPD fails to capitalize on opportunities to enhance the technical proficiency and professionalism of its officers. Whatever the ultimate impact, the lack of feedback loops from the field to the training function and vice versa is a deficiency.

Supporting Recommendation

Introduce an automated learning management system as discussed in Appendix I.

Further, the LAPD does not have an integrated learning management system or other information technology platform to handle training logistics such as course scheduling, instructor assignments, and facilities allocation. Although training data and documents are often in electronic formats, they are not housed in a single database or system. Personnel must piece together course materials, lesson plans, and trainee and instructor data from disparate sources in a very inefficient system. For example, the training organization could benefit greatly from an electronic master schedule that shows which instructors are teaching which courses on any given day and which students are assigned to each course.[46] Such a resource would considerably ease rescheduling in the event of an unforeseen instructor cancellation (e.g., due to illness). Beyond the basics of instructor and trainee

---

[45]Training coordinator focus group notes, November 14, 2002.
[46]Sutton and Murphy interview, 2003.

scheduling, a learning management system could also contain features such as scenario databases that could aid in curriculum development. While an effort to determine the personnel savings attributable to such automation is included in Appendix I, the full extent of such benefits is virtually impossible to measure without introducing such a system or conducting a very lengthy and expensive survey of current training management procedures throughout the Department.

The geographic dispersion of the Department's training facilities significantly affects how the Department uses its instructional resources. Between the two major components of the training group—the training division and the CED—training facilities are located in Elysian Park, Westchester, and Granada Hills. In addition, many of the ancillary training functions mentioned previously (e.g., training coordinators) are located at various sites throughout the city. There are considerable constraints on resource sharing and economies of scale in the training function because of the physical distance among sites and the related considerable travel time required to move between them. It is very difficult, for example, to have an instructor teach a continuing education course in the morning in Elysian Park and a Westchester recruit class in the afternoon without building in a significant amount of transit "downtime." Restructuring decisions obviously will need to take this factor into account.

In summary, the standing LAPD organizational structure is a design that may have worked well in years past but could benefit from changes that reflect an increased emphasis on police professionalism and integrated training approaches. Such changes would not only enhance training effectiveness but would also produce potential resource allocation efficiencies. Specific recommendations to achieve these objectives appear in the following section.

TRAINING ORGANIZATION RECOMMENDATIONS

The primary recommendation to the LAPD flows directly from the findings presented above; namely, that the LAPD should centralize authority for training curriculum development, training quality assurance, and instructor oversight in a single entity within the training group to ensure that Department values and standards of police professionalism are met. Several key findings would be addressed by this recommendation, including the lack of a central training management authority and the lack of continuity between recruit training and continuing education. Specifically, the LAPD should establish a training function—not a single staff member—subordinate to the commander-level head of the training group with development and enforcement authority regarding curriculum evolution; instructor selection, evaluation, and removal; and other critical tasks. The scope of responsibilities and workload would prevent the individual occupying the commander position from performing all of these roles. Centralizing authority and enforcement responsibility in an organization subordinate to the head of the training group would provide the commander with the resources to carry out all of the aforementioned tasks. A group of highly qualified personnel with extensive knowledge of police training, adult education methods, and related learning and development competencies could serve as a training oversight function with responsibility for quality assurance, instructor approval, and the maintenance of standards. It is recommended that the head of this organization hold the rank of a level-three captain or its civilian equivalent.

To reiterate a point made in the opening paragraphs of this section, the term "centralize" does not mandate the physical collocation of personnel. Rather, centralization implies the consolidation of authority in a single entity or organizational unit. As long as lines of communication are open and reporting relationships are clear, these personnel could conceivably be located in a number of different sites (an option made more viable by the introduction of significantly increased training group automation). In the proposed organization designs presented in this book, there are personnel who would report to a manager not envisioned to be collocated with those individuals.

We present two proposed designs that could fulfill this recommendation for consideration. Each is discussed in turn. (As noted, the reader should see Appendixes G and H for proposed organization structures and explanations of manpower reallocations.) The first proposed design, "Alternative 1" (see Figure 3.2), places the training oversight function under the auspices of the commander in charge of the training group and assigns it organizational status equal to the two major divisions that currently reside there in parallel (the CED

Alternative 1: Proposed LAPD Training Organization Structure

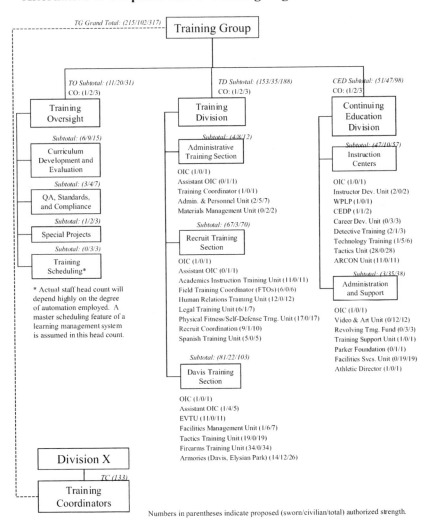

Numbers in parentheses indicate proposed (sworn/civilian/total) authorized strength.

Figure 3.2

and the training division). This design establishes a separate author-ity to handle all of the oversight roles previously mentioned. It has the advantage of preserving the function's autonomy and enabling it to provide services to all areas of training, whether recruit or in-service. Parts of the function's role—for example, scheduling—could be parceled out to other groups if deemed appropriate, but this risks losing some of the synergies that spring from housing all responsi-bilities together under the same reporting line. Instructors would still report to their respective divisions (the training division or the CED) or be drawn on a part-time basis as necessary from other areas, but the oversight function would have a mandate to manage them closely and make recommendations regarding their work. In addi-tion, the oversight organization could be given responsibility to manage the scheduling of students and instructors. This would allow top-performing instructors in a particular subject area to be better assigned to classes delivered in any part of the Department and would reduce the number of personnel engaged in schedule coordi-nation. However, this would result in a matrix-type organization for faculty members because they would report to their respective training division or CED leader while having to meet the demands of a schedule created by the oversight capability. Centralizing scheduling activities in the oversight function is contingent upon the implementation of a computerized master scheduling function.

Under Alternative 1, the total training group head count would de-crease from 329 to 317. Most of this reduction would occur as the result of elimination of redundant activities as well as from improve-ments in information technology. For example, the current organi-zation expends considerable staff time performing instructor/student coordination and scheduling tasks. Much of this effort will be eliminated through the establishment of a centralized scheduling unit and the implementation of a learning management system with master scheduling capabilities.

There are some significant changes from the status quo in Alterna-tive 1. Most notably and as discussed above, a training oversight function is established to centralize critical activities for both recruit and in-service training. The new training oversight function has four units under its authority: curriculum development and evaluation;

quality assurance, standards, and compliance; special projects; and training scheduling.[47] The LAPD may at some point find it advisable to form functional subunits under each of these groups as it refines the organization. Some of the support functions that were formerly in subunits of the CED or the training division would be subsumed by the training oversight function. For instance, consent decree and POST liaison units could be considered part of the new quality assurance, standards, and compliance subunit.

The CED has been reorganized into two sections, instruction centers and administration and support, to correct its current and somewhat arbitrary three-section division. The instruction centers focus on the delivery and coordination of continuing education programs. Administration and support consolidates all of the administrative functions performed in the CED. Total head count in the CED decreases in Alternative 1 because much of the "back office" training support work previously performed there has been moved to the new training oversight function. Consequently, the CED head count decreases from 130 to 98, with some of the work moving to training oversight. The reduction in head count represents not only the transfer of personnel to training oversight but also the elimination of duplicative work. It should be noted that there is an increase in one area of the CED: the tactics unit. The head count there is increased by 14 instructors and one supervisor to allow the LAPD to reduce its current in-service training cycle for tactics from five years to two years. This addition is also reflected in Alternative 2 below.

The training group's current police training and education is subsumed by the new training oversight function because its work activities closely mirror the charter of the new group. If this function retains its internal consulting role for all LAPD training programs, it might be considered a separate subunit of the training oversight function to preserve its autonomy.

The training division remains largely unchanged in Alternative 1 although there are a few minor changes in the administrative training section. Some support functions (e.g., evaluation and special projects units) have been subsumed by the new training oversight func-

---

[47]The names of proposed organizational units in this book are merely suggestive; the LAPD should select appropriate unit names as it proceeds with restructuring.

tion, and Westchester-based administrative support has been consolidated into a single administration and personnel unit. Even though the structure of recruit training is similar to the current state, the training oversight function will exercise authority over curriculum, delivery, instructors, and quality just as it will for the CED. The training division head count falls from 195 to 188.

Training coordinators remain in the divisions in Alternative 1 but will then have a "dotted-line" (functional) reporting relationship to the commander of the training group. This change reaffirms the training coordinators' responsibility for training delivery and signals to division management that training coordinators need to be relieved of some of their ancillary duties when they are required to teach. Because training coordinators are often an integral instruction resource—especially for continuing education and the CEDP module in particular—the new reporting relationship should be communicated throughout the LAPD.

A second possible restructuring design that facilitates central training oversight involves its consolidation in a unit that not only performs the functions described above, but also includes a host of dedicated instructors for both recruit and in-service training programs. This design appears in Figure 3.3 as "Alternative 2." Only the most basic administrative and support units would remain in the CED and training division areas; all full-time faculty would then belong to the training oversight function. This arrangement would allow the training group greater control over its vital instructor resources and would provide a dedicated staff of generalist and specialist instructors for all training levels.

In Alternative 2, the training oversight function would require a captain-level position or its civilian equivalent to lead its activities. The recruit section would also require a captain-level commanding officer (and most likely not a civilian position) because of the large number of recruits under his command. The support functions in the continuing education section could most likely be managed by a lieutenant-level position or a similar civilian position.

As in Alternative 1, the oversight function would be able to centrally manage curriculum development, quality control, audits, compli-

Alternative 2: Proposed LAPD Training Organization Structure

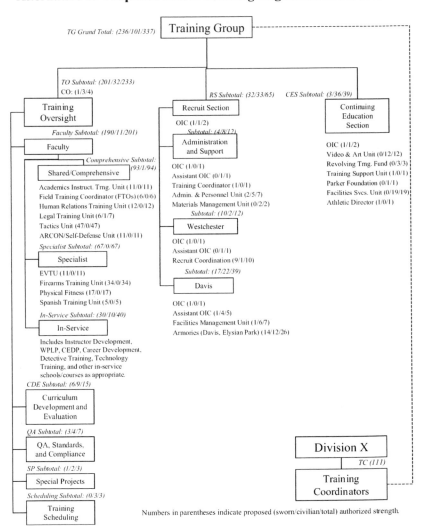

Numbers in parentheses indicate proposed (sworn/civilian/total) authorized strength.

Figure 3.3

ance activities, and scheduling processes. Many of the structural changes in Alternative 2 are also the same as in Alternative 1. Only administrative and support positions remain in the former training division (renamed the "recruit section" here) and the CED (called the "continuing education section"). Site-specific functions, such as armories and facilities management, remain under the control of these sections. All other work has been moved to training oversight. Consequently, the head count of the recruit section is now only 65 and the head count of the continuing education section only 39.

Alternative 2 departs from Alternative 1 in that the resources directly involved in teaching are moved entirely to training oversight. Training oversight has the same units as in Alternative 1, but with an added "faculty" function that has authority for all recruit and continuing education instructors. As the LAPD moves to an integrated training paradigm and strives to maintain professional standards in training, a centralized faculty corps such as this will greatly benefit the Department with increased continuity of policy messages, tighter adherence to standards, and resource flexibility. Within this faculty section are three subgroups: shared/comprehensive, specialist, and in-service.

The shared/comprehensive group would teach subjects that require broad knowledge of multiple elements of law enforcement. For example, arrest and control ("ARCON Unit") from the former CED would now report to the shared/comprehensive group because the training content involves a wide variety of policing issues that are relevant to both recruits and veteran officers, such as verbal communication and human relations skills, legal issues, and tactics. Ideally, the subunits of faculty under the shared/comprehensive unit would naturally consolidate over time as the LAPD moves toward a fully integrated training approach that values less "stovepiping" of instructors.

Recognizing that some skills are highly specialized and not as conducive to integration, there is a subgroup of "specialist" faculty. As proposed, this subgroup is composed of instructors for firearms and physical fitness. The subunits of the specialist faculty may vary, depending to some extent on technical factors.

Also, there is a third subgroup named "in-service." Although much of the training curricula associated with in-service training could well fall under the domain of the shared/comprehensive or specialist faculty, there may be some schools and courses under the continuing education umbrella that require distinct instructor staff because of the expert nature of the subjects (e.g., information technology or detective training) or other factors. In the final analysis, the LAPD may determine that the in-service differentiation is unnecessary and all faculty can be considered either generalists or specialists.

The faculty section has 201 personnel in total. This number includes all instructors from the former training division and CED as well as a new contingent of 40 dedicated instructors in the in-service category. These 40 "new" instructors are not necessarily new hires: Some would be drawn from the ranks of the training coordinators. In Alternative 2, in fact, 22 training coordinators have been transferred to the dedicated faculty section. Twenty-two training coordinators were chosen for transfer because this number reflects a percentage of the training coordinators who already perform significant instruction duties for the training group. Most of these training coordinators are located in the geographic divisions or bureaus, representing roughly 60 of the total of 133. Moving about one-third of these 60 coordinators out of the divisions would give the training group more dedicated instructors while still leaving sufficient resources in the divisions.[48] The remaining training coordinators would still report to their local commanding officers, but there would be a dotted-line reporting relationship to the commander of the training group. (Training coordinators would also be subject to oversight by the commander of the training group.) This way, the training coordinators can still be stationed in the local divisions but have the same quality assurance and oversight standards applied to them as the main instructor corps. Division management could still tap the training coordinators to perform some highly targeted, customized training programs for their local personnel, and their work emphasis

---

[48]Many of the geographic divisions have three or four training coordinators. Transferring one from each of these divisions to the training group—if his pedagogical skills merit such a move—would still leave enough training coordinators in place to carry out divisional training tasks, assuming their nontraining duties are not overly burdensome and there are no work shift constraints.

would shift away from administrative tasks to more-direct involvement in training and instruction.

Supporting Recommendation

Conduct an intra-Department analysis of training coordinator usage to determine how many positions should be assigned to the training group and how many others can be consolidated.

Two points are important in this regard. First, the number 22 is an estimate. It may turn out that a greater or smaller number of training coordinators can feasibly be moved to the faculty section after a detailed analysis of the current workload of these officers, an analysis beyond the scope of this study. (Such an analysis would logically also consider how to consolidate the remaining duties of various training coordinators in a manner that allows a reduction in the remaining number of such positions.) The analysis should be conducted by a disinterested party within the LAPD because reallocation of training coordinator positions will be very unpopular with those losing the slots. However, it is strongly advised that this reassignment be made. The current on-call nature of training coordinator support for CED instruction is inefficient and precludes the establishment and maintenance of the professional standards essential to achieving the quality of instruction sought by the Department. Second, it is this movement of 22 positions to the training group that accounts for the apparent advantage in "savings" of personnel Alternative 1 offers over Alternative 2. (Currently, the total strength of the training group under Alternative 1 is 317, and under Alternative 2, it is 337.) In other words, the Department does not save 20 positions by adopting Alternative 1 versus Alternative 2; the 22 training coordinators in question remain in the LAPD at large in the first case while in Alternative 2 they are assigned to the training group. The bottom line is therefore that the overall savings offered by the two alternatives are nearly identical.

Supporting Recommendation

Conduct further analyses of instructor positions, both before and after consolidation, to determine where additional redundancies exist.

The total Alternative 2 training group head count might be lower if further synergies in the ranks of instructors are found after consolidation. For example, after consolidating faculty, the LAPD might determine that there are seven instructors who teach essentially the same topics, yet demand requires only four such positions. A more detailed analysis that maps the number of instructors to the number of students in each subject area needs to be conducted.

It is worth repeating here that changes in reporting relationships do not necessarily imply the physical movement of personnel from one site to another. So, for example, if recruit instructors in Westchester now report to a training oversight authority in Elysian Park, it does not mean that the instructors are actually stationed in Elysian Park. The restructuring recommendations simply outline how lines of authority should shift to enhance lines of communication and improve both management and quality control.

Both of the proposed designs would achieve the ultimate goal of solidifying authority for training oversight in a group with the organizational leverage to introduce substantive change. The Department training function could then better ensure that consistent messages are delivered across training programs, whether they are in the training division, the CED, or elsewhere. For changes currently under consideration, Department specialized schools might or might not report to the training group. (Some proposals influencing this aspect of the training group structure were left open for consideration after the SOAR conference.) We strongly recommend that responsibility for the quality control of all such training be assigned to the training group even though instructors may in these exceptional cases remain with their original organizations. The training oversight function should still have the authority to manage course curricula and instructor qualification, evaluation, and retention. This recommendation will also assist the LAPD in its efforts to roll out less compartmentalized, more integrated officer training because it empowers a team of experts within the oversight function to closely monitor curriculum and classroom results.

As noted above, it is strongly recommended that the LAPD implement an integrated learning management system. Such a system would provide the training organization with an automated method of managing training logistics. The time required to perform work manually—for example, scheduling instructors—could be significantly reduced with the use of software. Centralization and consolidation of training resources and their attendant improvements in efficiency and effectiveness are virtually impossible to achieve without automation. There are many elements to consider in the design and implementation of such a system. Again, Appendix I outlines the range of options available to the LAPD with respect to learning management systems.

Chapter Four

THE POLICE RESPONSIBILITY TO COMMUNITY-ORIENTED POLICING IN A DIVERSE SOCIETY

Primary Recommendation

Integrate elements of community-oriented policing and diversity awareness training models throughout LAPD training.

THE REDEFINED POLICE PROFESSIONAL HAS A RESPONSIBILITY TO PUBLIC SERVICE

The professional man is a practicing expert, working in a social context, and performing a service, such as the promotion of health, education, or justice, which is essential to the functioning of society. The client of every profession is society, individually or collectively.... Financial remuneration cannot be the primary aim of the professional man.... The profession [is] a moral unit positing certain values and ideals which guide its members in their dealings with laymen. This guide may be a set of unwritten norms transmitted through the professional educational system or it may be codified into written canons of professional ethics.[1]

"Professionalism" for police today encompasses far more than the police professionalism model of 50 years ago. The earlier movement for police professionalism, more properly considered a police reform movement, had the effect of isolating police from the community, of-

---

[1]Huntington, 1957, pp. 8–10, 15.

ten to the degree that they were perceived as unresponsive and not sufficiently accountable to public needs. Such isolation was particularly apparent during the civil unrest of the late 1960s. Police might have been tactically or technically proficient in terms of their professional skills, but as a group they were not proficient communicators. Community-oriented policing (or community policing) and the community relations approach to policing, with its emphasis on police working with the community to solve problems, developed in reaction to the earlier professionalism-gone-wrong, or reform, movement.

Problem solving and community partnership have become valued aspects of police service since the time of the reform era. As one analysis notes, "Providing service to the community is the very nature of police work."[2] The LAPD's charge in fact is "to protect and to serve" the people of Los Angeles. Community policing and an awareness of community diversity are means to fulfill the responsibilities inherent in these tasks. As Huntington notes, the professional serves not himself but society. True police professionalism must therefore incorporate the duty of servicing the community.

It follows that law enforcement training has to account for the needs and increasing diversity of the communities police officers serve. An inherent aspect of that service is an officer's cultural understanding. Law enforcement personnel must understand and have an appreciation for the diversity of their communities and its implications for members of the police profession.[3] In an inherently diverse society, it is important for LAPD officers to understand the motivations and concerns of those whom they serve. Community representatives have expressed a willingness to help and a desire to work in partnership with police. In fact,

> community policing was the most frequent and articulate demand made by Los Angeles citizenry in the many public meetings, questionnaires and polls, as well as the Blue Ribbon Criteria Committee

---

[2] Peak and Glensor, 1996, p. 179.

[3] Shusta et al., 1995, p. 93.

deliberations of last summer in the process of selecting a new chief of LAPD.[4]

In this chapter, we review ways that the LAPD Training Group can better integrate community policing and diversity awareness with instruction throughout the Department, particularly with regard to use of force, search and seizure, and arrest procedures. The discussion begins by looking at how community policing has developed in Los Angeles and continues by identifying issues in community policing, problem solving, and diversity awareness in which the LAPD should seek to become more adept.

COMMUNITY POLICING AND ITS DEVELOPMENT IN LOS ANGELES

> To freedom-loving men, the Berlin Wall is an ugly welt upon the face of the world . . . [a] foremost symbol of lack of understanding among men and of brotherhood lost. Almost as impregnable and insurmountable, however is the invisible wall which separates many police departments and the citizens they serve. This wall, although not topped by barbed wire and embedded slivers of glass, still accomplishes the undesirable effect of thwarting communication between police and their communities.[5]

Community policing can bridge the gap between police and citizens by uniting them in a common effort to prevent and control crime. Community policing is defined as "a collaboration between the police and the community that identifies and solves community problems."[6] Ideally, such collaboration helps develop better relationships and mutual understanding between police officers and community members, which in turn help in solving community problems.

The most recent impetus for LAPD community policing in Los Angeles came from the recommendations of the Christopher Commission "that the Los Angeles Police Department . . . embrace a philosophy of

---

[4]Jones and Wiseman, 2003.

[5]Tamm, 1965, p. 10.

[6]U.S. Department of Justice, 1994, p. vii.

. . . *Community-Based Policing.*"[7] As part of the Department's community policing effort, officers and citizens participate in the following activities:

- *Community-Police Advisory Boards (C-PABs):* These boards involve police interaction with civilian volunteers from local area residences and businesses. The C-PAB advises the area commanding officer on crime and quality-of-life issues affecting the community. C-PAB members also present LAPD information to the community.[8]

- *Basic Car:* The LAPD comprises four operational bureaus (Central, South, Valley, and West). Each is divided into smaller community areas with its own police division, which total 18 throughout the city. Each of these community areas in turn is divided into eight to ten neighborhood areas referred to as "Basic Cars." There are a total of 168 Basic Cars throughout Los Angeles. Each Basic Car has one patrol car permanently assigned to provide service in that neighborhood. Each Basic Car also has a senior lead officer (SLO) responsible for establishing and maintaining police-community partnerships. SLOs are responsible for monitoring crime trends and special problems needing police attention, working with the local C-PAB and residents to develop goals for officers assigned to the Basic Car, and acting as liaisons with area detectives. A Basic Car district comprises groups of two or three Basic Cars. Each police division has a sergeant who directs and orchestrates the activities of the SLOs. This SLO supervisor provides a point of contact internally and externally for the individual SLOs.[9]

- *SLO Mentor Program:* There are two components to this program—SLO transition and SLO mentoring. The SLO transition component facilitates the transition between incoming and out-

---

[7]Parks, 1997, p. 1. [Emphasis in the original.]

[8]LAPD, Office of the Chief, Administration Order No. 6, May 18, 2000 (not publicly available).

[9]See www.lapdonline.org/community/basic_car_plan/bcp.htm, last accessed on March 11, 2003.

going SLOs. The SLO mentoring component provides aspiring SLOs exposure to the role and duties of an SLO.[10]

- *Area SLO Summits:* Area summits bring together key stakeholders from each area twice a year to identify the most significant problems in each of the 18 LAPD community areas.[11] The goal is to have those stakeholders assume a share of the responsibility for solving the identified problems through the formation of police and community collaborative teams or PACCTs.

- *Police and Community Collaborative Teams:* PACCTs consist of at least two SLOs, one or more community group representatives, and a representative from the local city council office. PACCTs are convened to address problems identified at area summits.[12]

- *Neighborhood Prosecutor Program:* The Office of Los Angeles City Attorney developed a neighborhood prosecutor program that assigned city attorneys to each of the 18 geographic areas. The role of these prosecutors is to focus on minor crimes and quality-of-life issues with particular emphasis on parks and schools. This program assists LAPD officers by serving as an important link between the Department and the courts.

- *Neighborhood Council:* Neighborhood councils promote community input into city government and help make it more responsive to local needs. As of February 2003, there were 60 neighborhood councils.[13]

- *Community Police Academy:* This ten-week academy is designed to give community members an overview of the LAPD's policies and procedures.

---

[10]Notice to all Sworn Personnel, from the Office of the Chief of Police, Subject: Senior Lead Officer Mentor Program, June 24, 2002 (not publicly available).

[11]Interdepartmental Correspondence to all Area Commanding Officers, from the Special Assistant, Subject: Area Summits and Police and Community Collaborative Teams (PACCTs), August 5, 2002 (not publicly available).

[12]Ibid.

[13]Intradepartmental Correspondence to all Area Commanding Officers, from the Chief of Operations, Subject: Neighborhood Council Update, February 11, 2003 (not publicly available).

- *Police Magnet Program:* This four-year program is conducted at five high schools and one middle school within the diverse communities of the Los Angeles Unified School District. The program identifies youth who have an interest in law enforcement careers. Approximately 1,000 youths are in attendance with annual graduation consisting of 120 students. Students participate in firearms safety demonstrations and take tours of the jail, juvenile hall, and the scientific investigation and the communications divisions. Students are also introduced to community problem-solving models and conflict resolution techniques.[14]

- *LAPD Online Web Site (LAPDOnline.org):* LAPD Online is the most comprehensive web site to provide frequently requested law enforcement and public safety information to those who live, work, and visit the City of Los Angeles. The site contains over 10,000 pages of general information and more than 1,000 Department publications for the public to download.

- *L.A. Community Policing Web Site (LACP.org):* LACP.org is the online forum for Los Angeles Community Policing. LACP is an independent organization dedicated to providing information about community policing, public safety, law enforcement, government, and criminal justice.

- *SAFE PARKS Program:* This is a joint initiative between the Department of Recreation and Parks and the LAPD to maintain a safe and family-oriented environment in the 385 parks within the City of Los Angeles.

- *Institutional Partnerships:* The LAPD has worked with the Pat Brown Institute to develop community policing and problem-solving training initiatives. It has also worked with the Museum of Tolerance to develop a course on "Tools for Tolerance" to enhance officer introspection about how personal prejudices or biases may affect interaction with the public.

Beyond these special initiatives, the LAPD has two internal entities for managing community-oriented policing efforts: the community policing unit and the community relations section. The community

---

[14]LAPD, 2003d.

policing unit provides information and training on community policing. The community relations section, established in 1965 in the aftermath of the Watts riots, strives to maintain open avenues of discourse between local communities and the LAPD regarding contemporary issues facing law enforcement.[15]

These efforts are impressive and commendable. Yet community policing is not a single program or group of programs. Rather, it is a policing philosophy of service to the community.[16] To realize the goals of community policing, the entire organization needs to reflect the goals and objectives of this philosophy. In short,

> community policing goes beyond simply implementing footbeats, bicycle patrols, or neighborhood stations. It redefines the role of the officer on the street, from crime fighter to problem solver and neighborhood representative. It forces a cultural transformation of the entire department, including a decentralized organizational structure and changes in recruiting, training, awards systems, evaluations, promotion, and so forth. Furthermore, this philosophy asks officers to break away from the binds of incident-driven policing and to seek proactive and creative resolution to crime and disorder.[17]

Unfortunately, the philosophy of community policing, as implemented in the Los Angeles Police Department over the past two decades, has often been less than clear. Community members and Department personnel alike were unable to articulate LAPD guiding principles for community policing. Chief Bratton states that "community policing is simple. It's the three Ps: partnership (with the community), problem-solving (with the community), and prevention (of crime in the community)."

---

[15]See www.lapdonline.org/organization/ocp/cag/crs/community_relations_main. htm and www.lapdonline.org/organization/ocp/cag/crs/ccpl_unit/acomm_cp_ liaison.htm, last accessed on March 11, 2003.

[16]Stevens, 2001, p. 8.

[17]Peak and Glensor, 1996, p. 75.

THE IMPORTANCE OF DIVERSITY AWARENESS

Los Angeles today is one of the most heterogeneous cities in the nation, with large Hispanic, African American, Asian, and non-Hispanic white populations (see Table 4.1). General U.S. population trends reflect this diversity. American society is ever diversifying, most recently because of Hispanic population growth. Between 1980 and 2000, the non-Hispanic population grew 16 percent, and the Hispanic population grew 142 percent. In Los Angeles the non-Hispanic population declined 8 percent between 1980 and 2000, while the Hispanic population grew 111 percent, spurring total city population growth by 25 percent.

Police work in Los Angeles cannot ignore the cultural diversity of the city or the speed with which its demographics are changing. The LAPD must train its officers to recognize cultural differences and barriers if it is to serve its people effectively. As noted in one analysis of law enforcement in multicultural communities, "The more professional a peace officer is, the more sophisticated he or she is in responding to people of all backgrounds and the more successful he or she is in cross-cultural contact."[18] Cultural and diversity awareness must include an understanding of cultural issues not only related to

Table 4.1

Los Angeles Population by Race

Race	Total	Percentage
Non-Hispanic, single race		
White	1,099,188	29.7
African American	401,986	10.9
Asian or Pacific Islander	369,334	10.0
Other	17,962	0.5
Non-Hispanic, multiracial	87,277	2.4
All Hispanics	1,719,073	46.5

SOURCE: U.S. Census Bureau, 2000.

---

[18]Shusta et al., 1995, p. 4.

race, religion, gender, and age, but also related to physical or mental disabilities and sexual orientation.[19]

There is disagreement about the most effective means for approaching diversity issues related to policing, but there are several guidelines to which police should adhere in addressing such issues. These include respecting and being sensitive to the needs of diverse communities. Further police training involving multicultural issues should be created in consultation with the communities. Diversity awareness has to be recognized as an integral aspect of policing philosophy as demonstrated in the conduct of field operations.[20] More specifically, training programs based on these principles should include instruction on

- various cultures in the community

- the effects of diversity on community relations and how best to deal with other cultures

- the ramifications of demographic and sociological changes for law enforcement

- the influence of perceptions, cultures, and prejudices on behavior

- public and private agencies that provide assistance to members of the community with special needs, such as immigrants

- reducing citizen complaints and lawsuits, negative publicity, and liability

- officer safety skills

- conflict resolution techniques

- how cross-cultural knowledge and skills contribute to "real police work."[21]

Developing officers who understand the nuances of policing in a pluralistic society and who can adeptly use this knowledge in their work

---

[19]Ibid., p. 92.

[20]Himelfarb, 1991, pp. 53–55.

[21]Shusta et al., 1995, p. 95.

is a constant challenge.[22] It can be especially difficult for a force that traditionally has prided itself on technical capabilities rather than on the full scope of effectual police techniques.

WHAT IS NEEDED FOR COMMUNITY POLICING TO SUCCEED?

Those responsible for training officers for community policing should be prepared to face stiff resistance. One of the common reasons for this resistance is a misunderstanding of the approach. Officers are inclined to think that community policing is "soft on crime." Department leadership and front-line supervisors need to actively work to overcome this misperception. Training must similarly target such misconceptions. Tactics that can help overcome misperceptions about community policing include conducting accurate community needs assessments, including all appropriate parties in collecting data to develop community policing strategies; assuring appropriate resources are available for community programs; and evaluating and modifying programs as needed.[23]

Supporting Recommendation

Make the LAPD a more "transparent agency," open to the entire community.

A police culture that cultivates an aura of secrecy also impedes the implementation of a community policing strategy. Too many observers contend that such a culture adversely affects the LAPD. One community member commented on his belief that the LAPD culture breeds an "end justifies the means" mentality and instills the "code of silence" in its officers.[24] A second concurs, noting that "the LAPD's so-called 'code of silence' exists as much today as it did when the Christopher Commission issued its report," contending that

---

[22]Himelfarb, 1991, pp. 53–54.

[23]California Department of Justice, 1999, p. 3.

[24]Community member interview by Estela Lopez, February 10, 2003.

Chief Bratton must make changing this problem his top priority if he wants to effect long-term change in the Department.[25] The insular attitude of such a "code of silence" perpetuates an "us versus them" mentality that inhibits collaboration between police and the community. In this context, Chief Bratton's goal of making the LAPD a "transparent agency" is imperative. Openness in the Department can generate trust and improved relations between the police and the community. Some feel policing cannot be truly effective without such trust.[26]

> **Supporting Recommendation**
>
> Develop and articulate a clear and unified message regarding community policing.

In case study interviews conducted in support of this project, respondents consistently noted that effective training hinges on police department leadership and commitment to training.[27] One law enforcement training manager noted that "a change [in] the training philosophy can't be made without an absolute commitment on the part of the chief and his staff."[28] LAPD officers indicated that community policing is being implemented inconsistently across Department divisions.[29] This variance in implementation might be attributed to the absence of a clearly disseminated message on community policing being promulgated by leadership, inconsistency in community policing training, leadership at lower echelons, or, most likely, a combination of factors. Unquestionably, clear and articulate guidance from the top is essential. Other initiatives are destined to failure without it. A new cornerstone upon which to build seems to be in place, but there is much building to be done.

---

[25]Community member interview by Estela Lopez, December 12, 2002.

[26]U.S. Department of Justice, 1994, p. vii.

[27]An overview of the case studies completed in support of this analysis appears in Appendix J.

[28]Harold Medlock phone interview, Charlotte-Mecklenburg Police Department, August 30, 2002, by David Brannan.

[29]Senior lead officer focus group, December 4, 2002.

Supporting Recommendation

Actively recruit diverse individuals who possess the appropriate values and skills necessary for community policing within diverse communities.

Department human resources policies, as an extension of guidance from the chief's office and a critical factor in using that guidance to direct training development, will also be crucial to the successful implementation of community policing.[30] Individuals are attracted to a career in the LAPD for a variety of reasons. It has been noted that while some see it as a way to make the community a safer and better place, others seek to become police officers because of the job stability or pay that accompanies the position.[31] Law enforcement agencies wishing to succeed in community policing cannot leave human resource development to chance. They must actively seek individuals with appropriate values and skills, hopefully those "with some exposure to college . . . who are ethical, responsible, and have a record of using good judgment in their discretionary decisions" and are able "to communicate effectively with an even temper, empathy, helpfulness, and a positive outlook and [to] establish a rapport with diverse groups."[32]

Some agencies undertake special recruitment programs in an effort to improve relationships with diverse communities. For example, the LAPD has a specific hiring goal for women. Other agencies have adopted residency requirements to ensure that they hire officers who reflect the community and its interests.[33] Those interviewed in the case study analyses suggested that diversity issues, particularly those regarding race, gender, and sexual orientation, are most effectively handled by actively recruiting officers from the communities of concern. Resulting community partnerships can help police "make the transition to facilitator of community needs and, through a positive

---

[30]Carter, 2003.

[31]Carlson, 2002, p. 122; LAPD probationers, FTO, and senior lead officer focus group notes, December 14, 2002.

[32]Carter, 2003.

[33]Carlson, 2002, p. 122.

relationship, work to achieve a desirable community."[34] The key, however, is officer competence. Promising candidates will have a multiplicity of the desirable characteristics mentioned in the previous chapters. Others will bring other significant assets to the Department. Quality officers on the streets begins with quality material entering academy training.

TRAINING FOR COMMUNITY POLICING

Supporting Recommendation

Train all LAPD personnel in the community-policing problem-solving model.

Effective community policing requires training for both police personnel and community members. Effective training aids the development of new police attitudes, knowledge, and skills and facilitates reorientation of perceptions and refinement of existing skills.[35] Many departments implementing community-oriented policing have developed specialized units or groups of officers. While this approach has had some positive results, it can also result in failure to involve and train other officers in the community policing skills they need. LAPD officers admit that community policing is currently limited to a chosen few and that many officers do not know what community policing entails.[36] Integrating community policing in Department training for every officer and having each perform community policing tasks are necessary to ensure the acceptance of community policing and its philosophy throughout the LAPD. As articulated by former Los Angeles Police Chief Bernard Parks,

> the fact is that responsibility for Community Policing is vested in about 191 members of this 12,000 member organization—168 Senior Lead Officers, 18 Areas captains, 4 geographic bureau commanding officers, and the Chief of Police. Supervisors, detectives,

---

[34]Stevens, 2001, p. 8.

[35]Peak and Glensor, 1996, p. 171.

[36]Multiple focus groups.

and even most officers assigned to the Basic Car Plan themselves feel little responsibility for the success of Community Policing . . . . Community Policing simply cannot be contained in a small room within each Area from which the SLOs work each day.[37]

Key Components of Community Policing Training

It is generally agreed that there are three key components to effective community policing: problem solving, community engagement, and organizational transformation. (The last element, with its focus on an organization's leadership, systemic issues, and structure, only indirectly affects training and thus is not included in the discussion below. Note, however, that adoption of a professional police ethic for the Department would fundamentally affect such a transformation.)

Supporting Recommendation

Consider adopting the CAPRA problem-solving model in lieu of the SARA approach.

Problem Solving. Problem solving is the practical application of community policing. Law enforcement agencies worldwide use many different problem-solving models. The most common is that used by the LAPD: SARA, or *scanning* for the problem, *analyzing* the specific elements of the problem, developing and implementing *responses*, and *assessing* the efforts made. SARA has been effective in many instances. However, some contend that it too often fails the agencies that use it.[38] Failures in SARA can often be traced to an insufficient emphasis on community involvement in the problem-solving process. As an alternative to SARA, the Royal Canadian Mounted Police have adopted CAPRA, or a model for understanding the *clients* (or *community*) and their needs and expectations, *acquiring* and *analyzing* information, establishing and maintaining *part-*

---

[37]Parks, 1997, p. 2.

[38]While there are other options, SARA has been reaffirmed as the primary problem-solving model in the state of California.

nerships for problem solving, *responding* to problems, and continually *assessing* performance.[39] CAPRA, by requiring police to consider solutions from outside the department, incorporates the second element of community policing: community engagement. (Presuming that the LAPD will retain SARA, training should ensure that appropriate emphasis is given to recognizing and understanding community needs during instruction on SARA in particular and throughout the curriculum in general. Emphasis on community needs is a primary point throughout the remainder of this chapter, as it has been in much of the material preceding it.)

Supporting Recommendation

Maintain, refine, and augment the LAPD's ongoing community engagement activities, including the citizen police academy.

Community Engagement. Contemporary community policing is based on the notion that all residents should be empowered to enhance their quality of life and prevent or eliminate crime and the problems that lead to crime.[40] Community members must be recognized for the vital role they play in accomplishing these goals.[41] Everyone benefits when community members understand the role and function of their police department and become active proponents of law enforcement.[42] The police must therefore educate community members about community policing and the role of community members in its implementation. The LAPD has made some effort toward this end. It needs to sustain and build on these initiatives.

One such initiative used by the LAPD and other police agencies is the citizen police academy. Citizen police academies have been effective in educating community members about the mission, goals, objec-

---

[39]Information from www.mts.net/`dcaskey/cp.htm, accessed February 28, 2003. Attempt to access this web site on May 28, 2003 failed—the web page is no longer available.

[40]Stevens, 2001, p. 9.

[41]Peak and Glensor, 1996, p. 40.

[42]Carlson, 2002, p. 115.

tives, and programs of the police department. They are typically offered free of charge and are open to any interested community member. Citizen police academy courses should include instruction on communication with police officers, including how words, actions, attitudes, and even tone of voice can affect an encounter with the police.[43] The LAPD Community Police Academy should retain this popular program and strengthen efforts to include all interested members of the general public.

The community can also contribute directly to community policing by developing or providing training. For example, the Citizen's Committee for New York City Neighborhood Anti-Crime Center developed and conducted a 25-hour community policing and problem-solving training curriculum. Producing such a curriculum allows the community to help define its role and that for officers in community policing. The LAPD has created opportunities for community input as well. A professional advisory committee of educators provides input on curriculum topics. As noted in institutional partnerships, the Department has collaborated with local organizations to develop area-specific training in community policing and diversity awareness.[44]

Police training of community members, such as can occur through community police academies, needs to help residents understand why police cannot successfully handle all crime and how a collaborative approach to problem solving leads to more effective crime control. Police officers should in turn be encouraged to develop a community profile or "beat book" identifying local leaders and resources. Officers should be skilled in communicating with the community through newsletters and public meetings with community leaders, groups, or other representatives. The circle becomes complete when the police and community members create meaningful roles for volunteers in working with the police to improve public safety.

---

[43]Peak and Glensor, 1996, p. 90.

[44]Greene interview, 2003.

Points of Inculcation

Training regarding community policing should provide officers with a level of understanding that will allow them to effectively use problem solving and community engagement techniques in their daily work.[45] More specifically, such a training curriculum should

- provide participants with an overview of the history of policing and of research on the community policing approach, including case studies where it has succeeded

- teach basic problem-solving skills and the elements of community engagement

- require officers to develop and work on a community policing problem

- demonstrate the benefits of collaborating with other government agencies, businesses, social service organizations, and the community

- explore the changes in leadership, management, and supervision styles needed to implement community policing.[46]

Such a curriculum should include some of the following activities that are typically part of a community-oriented police officer's day. In addition to traditional law enforcement activities, such as patrol and responding to calls for service, the day might include analyzing and solving neighborhood problems, meeting with community groups, working with citizens on crime prevention programs, meeting with local merchants, making security checks of businesses, and dealing with disorderly people.[47]

For this study, we assessed the current community policing training models used in the recruit academy, in field training for officers, and in continuing education (or in-service) training. We gave special attention to training on diversity awareness regarding persons of dif-

---

[45]Peak and Glensor, 1996, p. 178.

[46]Ibid.

[47]Mastrofski, 1992, pp. 23–27.

ferent race, sex, ethnicity, religion, and sexual orientation, and persons with disabilities.

Our findings are based on classroom observations, analysis of course curriculum, and interviews conducted with training and other police personnel, and external stakeholders including community members and elected officials. Overall, we found that

- the Department needs more training on community policing, problem solving, and diversity awareness
- community policing, problem solving, and diversity awareness need to be more thoroughly integrated into training (rather than taught in separate, stand-alone blocks as has been suggested in previous studies)
- classroom scenarios and case studies should be more carefully crafted to reflect real-life community dynamics that officers are likely to encounter (i.e., diverse groups of people with a variety of problems)
- the facilitation of classroom scenarios and case studies needs to better emphasize a problem-solving approach and application of problem-solving skills
- recruits should participate in community policing activities with their FTOs
- training involving participation by community members should increase.

Below is a review of more specific findings regarding training for the recruit academy, the field training officer program, and the continuing education division.

Recruit Academy. Experiences at the recruit academy can shape how well an officer will perform police tasks, including those of community policing, throughout his career. As one study of community policing notes, "the academy sets the tone for newly hired officers. It is at the academy that recruits begin to develop a strong mind-set about their role as police officers."[48] Another warns that

---

[48]Peak and Glensor, 1996, p. 174.

without changes corresponding to broader changes for community policing, recruit training "will be insufficient and doom the long-term goals of" community policing.[49]   Below are specific recommendations for improving elements of recruit academy training to support the broader goals of community policing.

The LAPD offers a two-hour course on community policing and problem solving in learning domain (LD) 3 "Community Policing" during academy instruction. This is the only community policing–specific course offered to recruits. Its instructor excels in defining community policing, communicating the responsibilities of community-oriented police officers, describing the SARA model, outlining community expectations of officers, and explaining means to overcome barriers between officers and the community. Overall, the brief course offers a good introduction to community policing. It can be improved. The course is far too short and does not offer enough time for recruits to practice their newly acquired skills in problem solving in scenarios or case studies. Its discussions of diversity awareness are too general. The role of management in community policing is not addressed at all.

Supporting Recommendation

Increase the length of the community policing course and use it for induction purposes.

The curriculum for the course has been condensed from comprehensive material that was originally covered in a six-hour course. We recommend that, at a minimum, the LAPD restore this course to its original length and place it early in the academy training. New recruits need immediate reinforcement that this issue is crucial to the Department. Many new recruits do not naturally know how to talk with residents in the role of LAPD officer. It is critical to provide early and solid training in communication, not only to defuse tense incidents, but also to train new officers to successfully work with merchants, attend neighborhood council meetings, and otherwise

---

[49]Stevens, 2001, p. 109.

interact easily and effectively with members of the Los Angeles community. New officers should be taught not only how to deal with negative scenarios, but also how to establish effective communications with citizens during routine interfaces. Failure to provide such training means officers will miss opportunities for positive interaction with constituencies who traditionally like the police and who could help strengthen police-community ties.[50]

Supporting Recommendation

Adopt as permanent the ongoing trial of introducing the basics of community policing and diversity awareness early in academy training and integrate community policing, problem solving, and diversity awareness throughout pertinent recruit instruction. Broaden this effort through field training and continuing education.

Even such a lengthened course is good only for introduction purposes. It should be followed by the insertion of community policing issues throughout the Department's training curriculum. Guidance from the Bureau of Justice Assistance concurs in this regard, noting that "community policing skills should be integrated into the training curricula, not treated as a separate component of the training program."[51] The LAPD is already undertaking such integration on a trial basis. In addition, the name of LD 3 as community policing is a recent POST change (the former name was tactical communication). POST also recommends that course presenters throughout the state offer the course during the initial week of academy training. Integration of community policing throughout other courses is not only theoretically sound, it will enhance, rather than supplant other POST-required material.

Diversity awareness training is currently taught in two learning domains: LD 42 "Cultural Diversity/Discrimination" and LD 37 "Persons with Disabilities." Both are comprehensive in the coverage of their topics. LD 42 includes discussions on issues of racial and ethnic

---

[50]Community member interview with Estela Lopez.

[51]U.S. Department of Justice, 2003, p. 36

diversity, special populations (including persons with physical disabilities, hearing and vision impairments, and mental illnesses), sexual orientation inside and outside the Department, and gender equity inside the Department. It also covers guidance on how to overcome personal bias and definitions of discrimination, stereotyping, prejudice, culture, and other pertinent concepts. LD 37 provides more detailed instruction on issues related to persons with disabilities. Both LDs do a fine job regarding how to deal with diverse groups of people. To do otherwise is to fail to properly prepare officers for situations they will confront in the field.

Supporting Recommendation

Involve recruits in problem-solving projects and encourage recruits to participate in various community activities during the training period.

As is the case with community policing, however, discussing diversity awareness in isolated classes is insufficient. A keen awareness of how to interact with different persons must be fostered and practiced throughout the curriculum. Diversity awareness should be integrated into all other learning domains. After these introductory courses on diversity awareness, recruits should have repeated opportunities to learn about the nuances of the community they will be serving as well as opportunities to discuss issues such as personal bias, prejudice, and discrimination. Tactical training programs such as those on use of force, arrest procedures, and search and seizure should also include training on dealing with diverse groups of people.

Community policing requires a decentralized approach to law enforcement, one in which operational and tactical decisionmaking is encouraged at lower echelons in an organization.[52] Recruits therefore need to be taught how to think independently and make decisions on their own. Such training will instill the confidence needed for them to be appropriately confident in their ability to initiate problem solving during interactions with their community. Cur-

---

[52]Peak and Glensor, 1996, p. 17.

rently, the LAPD and many other law enforcement agencies employ a military style of instruction that fails to promote decisionmaking skills and autonomous operations.

Supporting Recommendation

Develop problem-based scenarios and case studies that allow recruits to apply problem-solving skills and knowledge of diverse populations.

An excellent method of integrating community policing and diversity awareness training elements into all learning domains is the use of real-life, problem-based scenarios and case studies. A detailed discussion about the development of scenarios follows in the next chapter. Here, we reinforce the finding that the scenarios and case studies currently used by the LAPD are not explicitly problem-based and lack sufficient examples of real-life issues faced by the community. By working through a more problem-based curriculum, recruits will

- learn and use the steps of the problem-solving model
- discover the importance of thoroughly analyzing a problem using a variety of information
- apply the methods and resources involved in problem solving
- understand the value of problem solving to policing.[53]

Supporting Recommendation

Base the training approach on the tenets of adult education, promoting decisionmaking ability and initiative within the community.

Training should involve recruits in SARA (or preferably CAPRA) projects and encourage them to participate in various community activities during the training period. As noted, the LAPD has a number of community policing activities (e.g., area SLO summit meetings,

---

[53]Ibid., p. 182.

SARA projects, and neighborhood council meetings). Currently, recruits are not required to participate in ancillary activities with the community, a situation that should change. Our case studies indicate that other police departments encourage community involvement by recruits in a variety of ways. The San Francisco Police Department sponsors field trips for trainees to community gatherings and events. Other agencies encourage recruits to develop neighborhood portfolios, or beat books, which include identification of community groups and issues, advisory boards, and other resources for advice on solving problems encountered on patrol.[54]

Supporting Recommendation

Involve recruits in area SLO summit meetings and use qualified SLOs for academy training.

Since SLOs are the only officers who currently engage in community policing on a full-time basis, they are the ideal candidates to train new recruits about the application of community policing and problem solving strategies. SLOs are currently not involved in training at the academy. We recommend that SLOs be used as instructors or facilitators in academy training after their successful completion of the Department's instructor course. Note, too, that SLOs are a logical group to be trained in the problem-based learning model.

It is worth considering increasing the use of civilian instructors and guest speakers from the community. Civilians are rarely used as instructors or invited to be guest speakers at the training academy. The LAPD could benefit from using cultural, ethnic, or other group specialists as instructors and guest speakers. Selecting these speakers would require a screening process to ensure that those invited present a variety of ideas rather than advocating limited personal agenda, and that they meet Department instructor standards.

Field Training Officers. FTOs are important for solidifying the ideals of community policing throughout the force. The FTO has a tremendous impact on how the recruit views policing and, as a result, how

---

[54]See Appendix J.

that recruit will perform upon completion of his probationary period.[55] FTOs should reinforce academy lessons by helping the recruit put into practice the various methods and strategies learned during training.[56] Without FTO acceptance and espousal of a community policing philosophy, new officers will rarely put community policing into practice. Our recommendations for the FTO training program, which encompasses both training courses for FTO candidates and the role of the FTO in training probationers, are similar to those for the recruit academy.

It is suggested that the training group integrate elements of community policing, problem solving, and diversity awareness training, including working with special populations, into the FTO course, and involve FTOs in recruit academy instruction. As has already been suggested for probationer instruction in general, FTOs should be taught how to complement academy training in these areas. The Department might find it valuable to study the FTO program in Reno, Nevada, for potential lessons of value. The Reno FTO program ("post-academy police training") features a unique training relationship in which FTOs act as coaches and developers for recruits. The program is problem based, builds on what recruits are learning in the academy, and reflects their future work. Participants are taught further about problem-solving strategies during their post-academy field training.[57]

Continuing Education Division. In-service training or continuing education provides additional opportunities for reinforcing skills acquired in the academy and the FTO program and for maintaining skills in community policing and problem solving. In-service training is one of the primary means of introducing community policing to those trained and experienced in traditional policing.[58] It can also serve as a forum for discussing existing community problems, demographic changes, and changing community needs. There are several means by which the LAPD could improve its continuing education for community policing.

---

[55]Peak and Glensor, 1996, p. 175.

[56]Ibid.

[57]Hoover, Cleveland, and Saville, 2001, pp. 175–189.

[58]Peak and Glensor, 1993, p. 170.

Community policing and problem solving are not explicitly covered in continuing education programs. Only a two-hour block of training in community policing is offered in "supervisory school." This training course does an inadequate job of facilitating problem solving and neglects to discuss specific community expectations. The course also fails to present or apply problem-solving models.

Diversity awareness training is minimally addressed in the LAPD Continuing Education Delivery Plan (CEDP). Cultural diversity and tactical issues related to dealing with persons with disabilities are implicitly covered in the scenarios for CEDP I, an eight-hour training block for updating the field officer on a variety of tactical and non-tactical issues, such as vehicle stops and arrest techniques. Diversity awareness and discrimination prevention receive some coverage in CEDP V. In addition, a "Diversity and Discrimination in the Workplace" course is offered in supervisory school and detective supervisor school. While we did not observe or review these courses, written curriculum materials reflect that they appear to offer adequate information about workplace diversity and discrimination.

Supporting Recommendation

Discuss existing community problems in class in addition to problem-based scenarios and case studies.

As with the other points of inculcation, RAND recommends that the training group integrate elements of community policing and diversity awareness into all applicable training. Continuing education courses should use real-life, problem-based scenarios and case studies in all courses much as they are used in academy training. In-service programs should be a medium for officers to work through problems, or to share success stories, from the field. All training courses should help officers

- identify problems on the beat

- use the problem-solving model

- demonstrate an in-depth analysis of problems, including an understanding of environmental influences on the crime

- identify the diversity of resources available, variety of strategies to address problems, and crime prevention techniques

- simulate an evaluation of the process

- discuss the advantages and disadvantages of the process employed.[59]

Supporting Recommendation

Use SLOs as facilitators for training and consider increasing the use of civilian instructors and guest speakers from the community in training.

Neither SLOs nor civilians are greatly involved in continuing education programs. Both can help officers identify areas for collaboration with the community in solving local problems.

CONCLUSION

Police professionalism today goes far beyond "just the facts ma'am." It reinforces the fact that a police officer's prime responsibility is to serve the community. It is impossible to adequately serve a community without first understanding the community's needs and demands. It is therefore essential that law enforcement officials understand the cultures of the communities they serve.

Practical application of these philosophical tenets can only be accomplished through comprehensive, fully integrated training in community policing and diversity awareness. Individuals who possess the appropriate values and skills must be recruited to assist with the necessary training. All persons involved with the LAPD should receive training in which community policing and diversity awareness are integral parts and in which every problem challenges a student to consider issues relevant to these areas, just as they should during every interaction on the streets. The Department should enhance its existing partnerships with the community to strengthen the impact of training. Completion of these tasks will bring the LAPD

---

[59]Peak and Glensor, 1996, pp. 182–183.

closer to Chief Bratton's vision of community policing as the three Ps of partnership, problem solving, and prevention.[60]

---

[60]Bratton interview, 2003.

Chapter Five

DEVELOPING POLICE EXPERTISE

OVERVIEW

In 1977, political scientist William Ker Muir concluded that the essence of police work is coercion. Muir's argument is summarized in Fyfe et al. (1997, pp. 43–44) as follows:

> Like politicians . . . police are in the business of convincing people to do things they would not otherwise be inclined to do. . . . police face a major challenge in trying to avoid the use of force in their attempts to get others to behave in certain ways. . . . good police officers spend much of their time in skillful . . . manipulation of other people's behavior. The mere sight of a police car on the highway is a form of manipulation that slows would-be speeders. A blank stare from an officer in a pausing patrol car often can convince noisy corner groups of teenagers to take their parties elsewhere. . . . In some cases, like hostage negotiations or investigators' attempts to turn criminals against their colleagues, this coercion is very subtle and consists of leading suspects to recognize the decisions that they must make to serve their own interests. In other cases, as when officers make arrests or use deadly force, police coercion is far more overt and puts a quick and involuntary [for the perpetrator] end to wrongful behavior. . . . police coercion involves actual law enforcement. On most occasions . . . police change behavior merely by manipulating their subjects' knowledge that officers can always resort to law enforcement if inappropriate behavior is not changed immediately. Stated most simply, therefore, Muir's view is that good police officers are masters of legal coercion: the art and science of marshaling the authority of their office and their own personal powers to get other people to behave in ways the police define as appropriate.

Muir's view of police work was both insightful and prescient. It came at a time when the value of tactical communications was less formally appreciated than "hard" skills such as those involving weapons use or vehicle pursuit. His work foretold the broader expertise that many police officers would come to recognize as necessary to properly serve American society. Police officers today have to be expert both in hard skills of traditional policing and in communication skills. To communicate effectively is to be skilled in the overt and the subtle, to make one's intentions known whether the recipient is deaf, unable to understand English, mentally handicapped, enraged, under the influence of drugs or alcohol, or simply unfamiliar with normal police procedure.

In the past, training in the "hard skills" of policing sought primarily to improve physical prowess. An emphasis on only these hard skills of policing causes the officer on the street to be ill-equipped to meet the demands of public service today. To be sure, police officers continue to need the traditional skills of policing. To be responsive to today's needs requires integrating community policing and diversity awareness throughout training and understanding that use of force, arrest procedures, and search and seizure require a skillful blend of communications and physical ability. The focus here is therefore how best to imbue today's police officer with the totality of the expertise needed to serve society well.

Expertise, one of the defining characteristics of a profession, is the ability to master particular skills and apply them in a human context.[1] The professional acquires expertise by "prolonged education and experience."[2] The specialized knowledge and acquired skill of a professional are what sets him apart from others; in turn, "the expertise of the officer imposes upon him a special social responsibility."[3]

Professionals understand the need to gain and maintain proficiency as the demands of their profession evolve. The officer who does not maintain his expertise can sacrifice his status as a professional. Maintaining that expertise is a responsibility both of the professional

---

[1] Huntington, 1957, p. 15.

[2] Ibid., p. 8.

[3] Ibid., p. 14.

organization and of the individual himself. For their part, police department managers have a duty to provide continuing education and to encourage their personnel to consistently improve themselves.

The expertise of police professionalism, as has just been noted, includes both expertise in skills such as firearms proficiency, proper arrest procedures, and vehicle pursuit tactics as well as expertise in communication skills to help the officer persuade others without resorting to force. A good police officer is able to communicate effectively even under conditions of extraordinary pressure and stress. When such an alternative is feasible, the officer is a better servant of the people than one who is equipped only to employ overt force. The ability to combine physical adeptness and tactical communications proficiency allows an officer to accomplish tasks impossible with physical abilities alone.

A professional police officer has to adapt his skills to the ever-changing environment of his workplace. Law enforcement is a constantly evolving vocation the members of which must adapt to the dynamic conditions of the street. Comprehensive training that prepares the student to improvise in unpredictable situations is essential. As the New York City Police Department's deputy commissioner for training writes, "training for any endeavor should simulate as closely as possible the actual working conditions for which trainees are being prepared."[4] It is a statement with which virtually any educator would agree.

One way that training can best mimic the realities of the field is by integrating topic areas that are linked in real life. The officer who has been well trained and holds an integrated conception of the material he has learned is better able to recall and apply what he has learned during his service to the community. Being well prepared helps an individual improvise in resolving situations.

Such expertise is nowhere more important than in dealings with members of the public under circumstances that may threaten the lives of civilians or officers in an interaction. Use of force, search and seizure, and arrest procedures, the focal points of this study, are intricately related. Officers most expert in melding physical and com-

---

[4]Geller and Toch, 1996, Chapter 8, p. 7.

munications skills are those most able to bring events involving these focal points to a successful resolution.

Law enforcement agencies increasingly understand how complex those required communications talents are. The communications assets needed include far more than speaking eloquence. Verbal messages are influenced by nonverbal behaviors. The LAPD officer of today has to understand how to deal with the vast diversity that characterizes his city and to do so under the most demanding of circumstances: those involving use of force, search and seizure, and arrest procedures.

USE OF FORCE, ARREST PROCEDURES, AND SEARCH AND SEIZURE AS ISSUES OF EXPERTISE

Officers use physical force in fewer than one in 2,500 calls for service, but the use of force remains a critical issue in preserving civilian rights and protecting the lives of public servants.[5] Furthermore, because it is the rare instance when officers' employ *excessive force* that attracts media attention, justifiably ignites public debate over police abuse of authority, and impugns the professionalism of the department involved, police departments need to be especially concerned about how force is used and perceived.

How to properly exercise use of force, make an arrest, or conduct a legal search and seizure are fundamental to fulfilling an officer's responsibility to the public. They are also elements of police expertise used to enforce the law. The three are inextricably linked as an officer progresses through the course of his career. The responsibility bestowed on the officer necessitates specialized training to meet the demands of these areas without violating the rights of community residents.

To be sure, force can be required to safeguard the rights of civilians. As has been noted, "the very term *law enforcement* contains the word *force*." Because application of force is at times necessary for public safety, California law gives peace officers many carefully considered

---

[5]International Association of Chiefs of Police, 2001.

legal options for using force in doing their jobs.[6] Among these are giving verbal commands; employing control holds; using batons, pepper spray, or a canine unit; and the threat or use of deadly force, including drawing and discharging a firearm.[7] Most police departments have some form of "reactive control model" to assist officers' decisionmaking in this regard. This model is generally a part of a departmental use-of-force policy that outlines legal force options and instructs officers on behavior regarding use of force.

The LAPD and other departments nationwide have adapted their use-of-force policies and procedures to the changing demands of policing. During the 1960s and 1970s, for example, officers were required to modify their enforcement methods when "the drug culture produced hallucinogenic and mind-altering substances that confounded traditional force applications and resulted in significant increases in street level violence."[8] Policies changed again when "the 80s produced tremendous increases in gun-related violence" and officers were faced with "urban terrorists, operating at will with quality assault firearms, enhanced mobility, and improved tactics."[9] Today, as always, the police officer is best able to serve the community if he is able to adjust to situations and use his expertise to react appropriately under any circumstance.

Los Angeles has had its own unique incidents prompting concern over the use of force. The videotaped beating of motorist Rodney King by LAPD officers in 1992 caused a reexamination of legitimate applications of police authority across the country. The acquittal of the officers who were accused of the beating triggered rioting, looting, and other violence and chaos. Such crises reinforce public concern about preserving individual rights and raise vital questions about effective and legal policing, including those regarding variations in the treatment of different racial, socioeconomic, or gender groups. They also lead to demands for clear use-of-force guidance and call attention to the need for training that helps police officers

---

[6]Callanan, 1992, p. 17. [Emphasis in original.]
[7]Gillespie, Hart, and Boren, 1998, p. 3.
[8]Callanan, 1992, p. 19.
[9]Ibid.

understand the rights of civilians and the duties of police to uphold those rights.

Search-and-seizure and arrest issues are no less critical to policing than are those pertaining to use of force. The former have their basis in the Fourth Amendment of the United States Constitution. This amendment holds that

> the right of the people to be secure in their persons, houses, papers, and effects, against unreasonable searches and seizures, shall not be violated, and no Warrants shall issue, but upon probable cause, supported by Oath or affirmation, and particularly describing the place to be searched, and the persons or things to be seized.

The limit placed on police power by the Fourth Amendment guarantees the right to privacy for American citizens and is the "bedrock of search and seizure law."[10]

The laws and other legal guidance related to search and seizure and arrest procedures are constantly evolving. The changes highlight why police need refresher training in the practice of legal and ethical searches, seizures, and arrests. The tenet of professional expertise requires (1) that every officer understand the foundations underlying pertinent fundamental rights, (2) that he comprehend the laws and court decisions designed to protect those rights, and (3) that he be aware of changes to those laws and decisions that affect the execution of his duties in support of society. This understanding establishes only a foundation. Training has to help officers to build on this base by developing the communications skills and judgment that ready them to apply their knowledge in dealing with even the most unexpected of challenges on the streets.

Primary Recommendation

Develop training on use of force, search and seizure, and arrest procedures that meets current standards of excellence.

---

[10]NOLO Law for All, 2002.

Educator Benjamin Bloom wrote that "learning content is not enough. Learning how to use that knowledge, compare and integrate it with other pieces of knowledge, and evaluate its usefulness is the individual's responsibility."[11] Such is the task of the LAPD Training Group. Observations regarding adult learning and police education as described in Chapter Three offer some ways in which its accomplishment can be more effectively approached. Chapter Four discussed in detail two critical components of the educational context for virtually all instruction regarding use of force, search and seizure, and arrest procedures: community policing and diversity awareness. The discussion that follows builds on these earlier commentaries by addressing how those observations apply specifically to the three areas of expertise under consideration here. We present, in turn, four elements fundamental to successful training and consider how each influences the development of professional expertise:

- Contextualize the learning.

- Integrate key topics throughout the curriculum.

- Build the scenario.

- Conduct a thorough debriefing.

Unsurprisingly, many of the characteristics of good training necessary to better prepare police instructors presented in our earlier chapters also pertain to the educating of their students. Similarly, these four elements will greatly enhance the development of student expertise during academy instruction, in-service classes, and when the students are themselves prospective instructors.

Contextualize the Learning

Training and teaching that frame new information in the context of what is already known is called contextualization. Contextualization is a style of adult learning that seeks to tie new information to existing knowledge and real-life situations. It builds on students' experience and education in connecting the existing understanding and

---

[11]Evers, Rush, and Berdrow, 1998, p. 60.

new material. It recognizes that skills and knowledge are integrated in field application and therefore can be taught in a like manner.[12]

Contextualization is based on the premise that training should mimic real life or simulate "as closely as possible the actual environment in which the application of foundation skills occurs."[13] That is, the officer is trained in the same way that he will do his job. Using a contextualized or integrated approach in training recruits prepares them for the realities of policing better than providing techniques without an understanding of how to mix them in the field.   The LAPD recognizes the importance of contextualized scenario-based learning; its *Arrest and Control Instructor's Manual,* for example, notes that, "when an officer becomes familiar with the common patterns of combative resistance and learns simple effective techniques in realistic scenarios based on these patterns, that officer's experience and training are substantially enhanced."[14]

Supporting Recommendation

Use contextualization to enhance realism in training and enrich learning processes.

The scenario training for the "Law Enforcement Tactical Application Course" (LETAC) provides an outstanding example of effective contextualized situational learning in continuing education. Our seven hours of observation of LETAC training at Elysian Park Police Academy in November and December 2002 found scenario training to be conducted in a problem-oriented fashion in which students attempt to appropriately deal with situations presented by their instructors. The scenario training was well structured and implemented. Scenarios incorporated diversity and special-needs issues. The instructors presented real-life, challenging situations; and each scenario was complemented by a thorough debriefing session. This method of teaching integrates new learning material into an officer's

---

[12]Penn State College of Education, 2003.

[13]Ibid., p. 1.

[14]Dossey, 1997, p. 3.

existing knowledge and provides officers the opportunity to discuss information as they learn it.

One LETAC scenario dealt with a possible suicide in progress at a park. The officers in training were expected to approach this situation as if they had just received a radio call and arrived on the scene. To contribute to the realism of the situation, officers were given inert weapons and the scenario took place in a portion of the Elysian Park campus that resembled city park lands. After the officers and the suicidal subject (a role-playing officer) had resolved the scenario, another LETAC officer assisted in a debriefing to discuss what the officers did well and how they could improve. The lengthy and comprehensive debriefing session following each scenario reexamined ways that the officers could have communicated more effectively with the subject. This often led to a discussion of communication techniques. Most scenarios, like most police incidents, did not involve the use of force.

Officers participating in this training took the exercise very seriously and applied themselves in trying to resolve the situation. Students took advantage of the opportunity to reconsider their performance, including their integrated use of all police tactics. They recognized it would have been unnatural to isolate each topic and discuss it without acknowledging interrelationships. The student who gains a contextualized conception of how topics are related understands how he will be expected to use them in his job. Such training better prepares the officer to improvise and resolve any situation, both those practiced and others never previously experienced.

Integrate Key Topics Throughout the Curriculum

Contextualizing knowledge for the learner is closely related to the idea of integrating topic areas, which "recognizes that skills and knowledge are integrated (used together) in real life and should be developed and practiced in an integrated manner."[15]

Topic integration is strongly supported in the field of educational theory. The higher levels of learning—synthesis and evaluation—are

---

[15]Penn State College of Education, 2003.

based on combining various knowledge, facts, skills, and logic to make unique personal judgments. Recruits must be transformed into police officers who can combine and synthesize information in making legal and ethical judgments. In-service students need to continually refine that ability.

Supporting Recommendation

Use contextualized learning techniques to integrate topic areas in training curriculum.

Effective officers use information in a fully integrated manner in the field. Training should reflect this by drawing connections among multiple subject areas and thereby enabling the student to better understand the challenges of an officer's job. The officer should be trained to understand the relationships among the subject matter covered and the techniques that he will be using.

It is of little value to artificially separate subject areas. An officer will rarely find himself in a situation in which he has to make an arrest without also having to search the subject and contemplate the possibility of appropriate use of force. Problem-based and contextualized learning communicates information in an integrated fashion so that it can be better recalled and applied in an integrated fashion. Arrest, search, and use of force have unique tactical characteristics that in the context of professional service are best viewed as three parts of a whole.

As was alluded to earlier, there are some basic skills such as how to conduct pat-down searches, apply handcuffs, or fire a Taser that might be first taught independently and later integrated into more-comprehensive scenarios. Yet even in these instances, the new skill must be set in the context of other techniques, the laws and policies that govern their use, and relevant community policing and diversity issues. Even basic techniques for handcuffing an individual can differ, as might be the case for a subject under the influence of drugs or alcohol, wearing an arm cast, or one confined to a wheelchair.

Another example illustrating the importance of integrated training is that of an officer stopping an individual whom he suspects has contraband. The officer has to determine whether he has probable cause to make the stop. He then determines whether a search is warranted and, if so, the most effective technique for conducting that activity. While looking for contraband, he bears in mind the many safety standards to which he should conform for his safety and that of the subject and others in the vicinity. The officer has to remain aware and be prepared for use of force anytime during his arrest or search.

The LAPD has been creative in building learning domain instruction that connects disparate subject matter through ad hoc "surprise" scenarios. Such creative techniques can both reinforce skills integration and assist students in attaining readiness for any challenge with which the street might confront them.

An understanding of professionalism and its responsibilities points to five elements that, if incorporated throughout LAPD training, would move the Department well along the path toward meeting the dictates of the consent decree's paragraph 133. These overtly include elements of professionalism in training, considering the consequences of officer actions, contemplating lessons learned, maintaining student awareness of diversity and special-needs issues, and exercising community policing and problem-solving skills. Except for the last elements, the discussion below considers how each of these is currently integrated in the LAPD training curriculum and how it might be better integrated. Please refer to Chapter Four for the full discussion about community policing.

Professionalism. A good example of topic integration in recruit training curriculum is LD 31, "Custody."[16] It includes many of the primary issues that should be integrated into all training curricula, to include the tenets of professionalism. It makes clear the consequences when an officer neglects his responsibilities and incorporates diversity awareness issues so important to properly serving the public. Notably, it also integrates valuable insights drawn from lessons learned from the field.

One of the goals of the custody LD is to teach recruits their responsibilities when they take a citizen into custody. A section of the LD

---

[16]LAPD, Training Division, 2001a.

covering "Violation of a Prisoner's Civil Rights" teaches that "peace officers represent and symbolize the law. They have a special legal and professional responsibility to ensure that the civil rights of all citizens, including prisoners, are protected."[17]

Instruction provides specific examples to complement the general guidance. An officer learns that denying an inmate a phone call, neglecting to address a medical concern, and discriminating against the inmate are civil rights violations. The LD also emphasizes the officer's professional responsibility to protect the inmate from harm. This is an exemplary application of integrating the tenets of professionalism in training material. The officer is taught not only that his tactical skills, in this case how to take a citizen into custody, are a function of physical ability and protection of a suspect's rights, but also that their proper use is a professional obligation.

Consequences of Actions. The custody LD explicitly identifies the consequences of neglecting custody duties to reinforce the obligations of the student's status as a professional. Too many other LDs are vague or entirely neglect to discuss the consequences of extra-legal behavior. LD 16, "Search and Seizure," does not review the ramifications of an illegal search or seizure, for example.[18] LD 15, "Laws of Arrest," makes only general reference to the "potential civil liability/administrative discipline against the officer" engaging in civil rights violations.[19] LD 31, in favorable contrast, explicitly lists the penal codes that apply to officers who violate individuals' civil rights and specifically lists the legal and Departmental ramifications of such actions.

Communicating the consequences of intolerable conduct reinforces the importance that the Department places on appropriate and professional behavior. It clarifies the expectation that the officer will perform in-line with Department policy and the core values of the Department, serving citizens with the "highest ethical standards to maintain public confidence."[20] When such consequences are not

---

[17]Ibid., p. 9.

[18]LAPD, Training Division, 2001c.

[19]LAPD, Training Division, 2001b, p. 17.

[20]From LAPD, 2003b.

presented or accountability is unclear, perceptions of risk can be greatly skewed, leading to abnormal or excessive risk-taking, exaggeration of potential gains versus potential losses, and other critical decisionmaking errors. Ideally, training should focus not only on the specific legal consequences of violating policies, laws, and civil rights, but also on the professional reasons for not doing so in the first place.

Lessons Learned. As discussed at length in Chapter Three, lessons learned can be an important tool in developing training that replicates field conditions, providing officers with insight into the realities of policing and helping them prepare for whatever challenges the future might hold. LD 31 does well in incorporating lessons learned from the field into classroom learning material by describing common errors frequently seen when police take subjects into custody. A similar use of examples from actual events takes place in LD 21, "Patrol Techniques."

Supporting Recommendation

Use lessons learned to create realistic scenarios for classroom training.

Unfortunately the use of lessons learned in a negative context is the norm, as is the case in presenting "Common Errors" or "Ten Fatal Errors" during class sessions. Negative lessons undoubtedly have a place in the classroom for demonstrative purposes, but successful problem resolutions and other positive examples should also be used. Successes can be harder to identify because they typically involve the absence of notable events. Doing so is one of the objectives sought in establishing a formal lessons-learned structure within the LAPD.[21]

Diversity Awareness and Special-Needs Populations. Because of the diversity of Los Angeles, the LAPD officer needs to practice his skills under varied training conditions. Scenarios need to be realistic, seeking to confront students with situations at least as difficult as

---

[21]William Geller, expert panel proceedings, one-day workshop, Santa Monica, Calif., October 14, 2002.

those they will experience during field duty. Exercises should not shy away from recognizing potential shortcomings in students. As one analyst notes, "there is no reason to believe that prejudice is any rarer among police than among the general population."[22] Good training accepts such challenges and seeks to meet them head on. Well conducted, it might assist officers in defusing their hostilities and overcoming prejudices. Quality training sends a strong message that under no circumstances will officers be permitted to "act out their prejudices through violent, or even discourteous, conduct."[23] Incorporating diversity awareness issues in all aspects of recruit and in-service training provides a constant reminder of the public-service responsibilities inherent in every aspect of police work. Integrating such elements throughout LAPD curricula clearly communicates a Department commitment to just and legal treatment of all persons.

LD 31 is also a model for incorporating issues regarding diversity awareness and special-needs populations. It specifically calls for upholding the civil rights of each individual regardless of special characteristics such as race or ethnicity. It also has a section on "Prisoner Classification" that draws attention to particularities of the individual inmate, including the special needs of juveniles; alcoholics; drug users; inmates who are emotionally ill, mentally retarded, or otherwise handicapped; and sex offenders.

Officers need to understand that every public interaction is a unique event. For example, an officer trying to search a subject who is an alcoholic should be aware that this person is prone to severe tremors, disorientation, and possible convulsions.[24] The alcoholic may be less responsive than other individuals, or he may need physical support to stabilize himself while the officer conducts a search. Nearly half of U.S. traffic stops in which use of force was eventually used involved persons under the influence of alcohol or drugs.[25] Knowing how to determine that a subject is possibly experiencing problems due to alcohol withdrawal or drug use enables an officer to make better decisions about how to interact with the individual. For the offi-

---

[22]Geller and Toch, 1996, Chapter 8, p. 2.

[23]Ibid.

[24]LAPD, Training Division, 2001a, p. 17.

[25]International Association of Chiefs of Police, 2001, p. iv.

cer to best serve each citizen, he must be aware of such conditions so as to tailor his approach to ensure a mutually beneficial and safe outcome.

Supporting Recommendation

Complement recruit learning domains with specific communication techniques for diverse and special-needs populations.

Another positive aspect of LD 31 is its inclusion of a list of potential "prisoner classifications" that the officer might have to manage. The LD provides possible symptoms to look for among substance abusers, identifies persons who might be prone to assault by other inmates, and discusses populations that could pose a security risk. While increasing the awareness of the officer to such issues is important, it is equally important to give him strategies for communicating with diverse and special-needs populations. The LAPD needs further integration of communication techniques throughout its training curriculum. Use of lessons learned can be particularly helpful in developing effective instruction in support of such integration.

There is an immediate need for increasing the integration of demographic diversity considerations in LAPD training. Forty-one percent of city residents are foreign born; 58 percent speak a language other than English at home.[26] Nevertheless, LAPD training does not include instruction on communication when there is a language barrier between an officer and a civilian. Recruit training LD 15 on "Laws of Arrest" clearly states that the officer must administer Miranda warnings to a subject prior to taking him into custody. However, it does not provide protocol for situations when the individual speaks a language that is foreign to the officer, even though the LD recognizes one of the "elements of Miranda" is that the subject understands the warnings given by the officer. Such failures to provide adequate training for communication across language barriers can make arrest and use-of-force situations far more difficult to negotiate. Physical tactical procedures are thoroughly explained in LD 15 and in LD 20

---

[26]U.S. Census Bureau, 2003.

on "Use of Deadly Force," but there is no attention given to language barriers or demanding field situations. Police resources such as bilingual positions and the language bank available through the communications division should be clearly referenced in the curriculum.

Supporting Recommendation

Develop training on tactical communication in proportion to the frequency that it is used in the field.

An officer should be trained to understand how his personal state of being can influence his perspectives and performance of duty. A police officer's emotional and physiological states are likely far different when arresting a compliant individual than when apprehending an individual after a lengthy foot pursuit or high-speed vehicle chase. Training should provide guidance on when an officer ought to remove himself from the situation at hand and ask for assistance from others because of his own state of mind. It should similarly develop skills regarding how not to take interactions personally and how an officer can best control his emotions. Finally, effective instruction will recognize that police officers are part of a team. It therefore should cover a partner's responsibilities regarding minimizing the risk of excessive use of force by his fellow officer.

Elements of LD 3 on "Tactical Communications" should be integrated throughout the LAPD training curriculum to underscore the importance of tactical communication skills. The ultimate result should be that every officer's communication skills match if not exceed his physical skills mastery.

Build the Scenario

How are contextualized learning and integration of topics best applied in police training? Scenarios help align a curriculum with the main tenets of adult learning: learning by doing, reflecting real life, and making the learning interactive and self-directed.

Scenario training offers the dual benefits of grounding instruction in the known while introducing the new, thereby allowing the student to synthesize information and function at his highest level of learning. Scenarios by their very nature require integration of topics. Traditional classroom instruction, by contrast, often deals with topics discretely, does not require hands-on practice, and thereby leaves information abstract and compartmentalized in the mind of the student.

The process of learning how to drive a car illustrates how learning works and how topics learned discretely must eventually be integrated. A student wishing to obtain a driver's license must pass a written exam demonstrating his knowledge of traffic laws, that he understands the meaning of braking distances, and that he knows how to adjust for various weather conditions. It is not enough to read a car manual and its explanations of how the windshield wipers, turn signals, brakes, and steering wheel work. The student must practice by actually driving the vehicle under controlled yet realistic situations. Without such practice, the student cannot learn to anticipate the variety of situations that he might encounter on the streets. We would never accept that someone learned to drive adequately simply by reading a book. Use of contextualized learning and scenarios is supported by 30 years of educational research. Learning that is retained is that which engages, challenges, and involves the student.[27]

The Los Angeles Police Department has been working to integrate scenarios in more of its training courses. Newly developed Continuing Education Delivery Program modules are based almost entirely on scenarios. In-service courses such as LETAC and ARCON also incorporate them. The recruit academy is similarly increasing their use. These trends are positive ones in light of adult education best practices. Yet it should be noted that scenario use does not in itself lead to success in training. Scenarios are tools for replicating real-life situations. Only a few such situations can be covered in any curriculum. Instructors and curriculum designers should incorporate unexpected elements in their scenarios in recognition of this limitation

---

[27]Glickman, Gordon, and Ross-Gordon, 1995, p. 380.

to better prepare officers for the never-before-seen as well as specific events addressed during training.

Key Communication Elements to Include in the Scenario. The LAPD Continuing Education Delivery Program establishes a good initial foundation for further development of scenarios in support of Department training. There is room for improvement, however, particularly in adopting adult education principles for an integrated approach in recruit training. The variables discussed in Appendix K include those that should be considered when building training scenarios. The appendix does not provide an exhaustive list, but it does cover many of the issues that need to be considered in police training. The focus is an area requiring improvement for the Department: tactical communications.

Tactical communications are at the center of all police interactions with the public and are particularly critical for officers seeking compliance or cooperation from a subject. It has already been repeatedly noted that tactical communications therefore need to be considered in training for any police activity. Tactical communications as currently taught are too limited in scope and poorly integrated with other instruction. Explanations regarding the character of effective communications and how to employ them in the field too often border on the superficial. Whether a police officer is giving driving directions to a tourist, responding to a medical emergency, pulling over a speeding vehicle, or taking a violent felon into custody, he will need tactical communication skills if the outcome is to be positive. Public and officer safety are jeopardized by poor communications. An unarmed officer possessing well-honed communication skills would in many cases be a more potent law-enforcement implement than an officer with poor communication skills but expert in the use of weapons. The ideal combination, and the legitimate objective of Department training, is a balance between these two extremes: officers who are both skillful communicators and proficient in the use of physical assets.

Two premises should be reiterated at this point:

- *Equitable treatment does not necessitate identical treatment.* While everyone should be treated fairly and granted all the civil protections due them, communications can and should vary as necessary. A police officer must be able to alter his communication approach to suit circumstances. For example, in the interest of equal treatment, speaking to a deaf person who is unable to read lips would be ludicrous.

- *Small changes in communication methods can cause significant changes in the outcome of any interaction.* Knowing what changes to make in given circumstances is an essential ingredient in developing good tactical communication skills.

The Communication Continuum. Communications between police and the public do not take place in a vacuum. Training must therefore not treat them as if they do. Even a one-on-one interaction can have witnesses, either among bystanders or those who later see the interaction on videotape or hear about it from others.

Police officers serve in an environment with a communication continuum. Along this continuum are communications that are characterized as follows:

- *Primary*: between the officer and an individual or small group and those in the immediate vicinity who witness the interaction.

- *Secondary*: between the officer and those who witness an interaction from a more distant perspective such as across a street or through a window. If some component of the primary communication is missing—for example, if only part of the communication is witnessed or not all of the words exchanged are heard—then it is secondary.

- *Tertiary*: officer communication mediated by a newspaper, a televised report, or as recalled by a bystander.

Police officers should recognize that their tactical communications extend beyond their primary focus into secondary or tertiary realms. Moreover, secondary or tertiary factors can influence the primary communication, as when hostile bystanders affect the behavior of a subject being interviewed by an officer.

The Variables in Persuasive Communications. Effective communications are tailored to the circumstances at hand. This is especially true of persuasive communications. Voluntary compliance is the result of successful persuasive communication. The literature of social psychology recognizes a number of variables that contribute to the outcomes of persuasion efforts. Ignoring or inadequately addressing these variables will thwart any effort to obtain voluntary compliance. Conversely, the best persuaders employ these variables skillfully and are rewarded for their efforts.

A listing and discussion of some fundamental persuasive communication variables that are important to police tactical communications appear in Appendix K. These are drawn from the seminal texts and reports on persuasive communications. They are grouped into four categories for ease of use:

- the *source* of the persuasion attempt
- the *subjects* of the persuasion attempt
- the *environment* in which the persuasion is attempted
- the *format* of the persuasive message.

Although the appendix is not exhaustive, it covers most of those variables found in the literature of social and cognitive psychology to contribute greatly to the outcome of persuasive communication attempts. The variables should be treated as a foundation for communications used during interpersonal interactions and subjected to evaluation during scenario-based exercises. Relevant questions might include the following:

- Which variables are most—and least—important to the police officer in such cases? For example, which few are most important for a recruit to remember in seeking voluntary compliance?
- What other circumstances (e.g., time of day, weather, condition of subject, and number of officers) can influence the use or effectiveness of a variable?
- How does the value of variables change? For example, is it correct to assume that if the individual is intoxicated the officer can forget about speech pattern as an indicator of attitude?
- What variables can the officer control (e.g., the amount of time given to a subject to consider a command) and how should he control these? How should an officer react to variables he cannot control (e.g., language barriers)?

Conduct a Thorough Debriefing

Scenario training should be accompanied by thorough debriefings. Debriefings often receive short shrift in the training process, but they are critical to solidifying learning. Assistant Chief George Gascón notes that "because scenario training can be open-ended and less controlled than lecture, it is essential to bring things together at the end." [28]

We observed inconsistencies in LAPD training debriefings; several instructors appeared to have difficulties guiding and concluding them. Instructors need to practice breaking down what the recruit is learning using a structured, detailed, and consistent format—a debriefing that consistently follows the same format and reviews similar key elements of instruction (e.g., What were the subjects' demographic and psychological descriptors? What was the background noise like during the event? How many bystanders were there and how might they be characterized?). Creating standardized debriefings will provide a critical benefit to training. Effectively conducted, they should improve student performance. A student who knows what he or she will be debriefed on will pay more attention to those details during the interaction, thereby improving both performance and recall of salient details. [29]

Debriefings should be constructed at the same time and in the same way that a scenario is built. This simultaneity allows the curriculum developer to identify the learning points that he wants to cover, incorporate them in the scenario, and ensure they are reinforced during the debriefing session.

Debriefings in the field should follow the same format as those in training, thereby increasing the transfer of knowledge from classroom to field and back again. Conducting debriefings in a structured, consistent fashion will allow the LAPD to assess why and how communications techniques succeed or fail in the field. Without this kind of analysis, assessments are based on little more than opinion and hindsight.

---

[28]LAPD, 2001.

[29]Iyengar and Kinder, 1987.

The goal of scenarios is to practice decisionmaking and other skills as officers would use them in the field. Instruction can be ineffective or even detrimental if a session is not closed with a structured discussion about the relative merits of different actions (including actions that are illegal or unethical). An instructor has a duty to facilitate an active discussion among students and to clarify points as necessary.

CONCLUSION AND SPECIFIC RECOMMENDATIONS

We have suggested a process that can serve as a guide for building a curriculum that promotes successful Department training to meet the demands of establishing and maintaining police expertise. It consists of the following four elements:

- *Contextualize* training materials to give the officers a real-life understanding of what they are learning.

- *Integrate* key topic areas to demonstrate how they are related and how they will be used in policing.

- *Incorporate* scenarios based on lessons learned from the field throughout all Department curricula.

- Conduct *thorough and comprehensive debriefings* to provide immediate feedback on student performance and reinforce primary teaching objectives.

The goal of police training is not to provide officers with checklists of options or to exhaust the list of possible situations that they might confront by covering every possible event during instruction. Rather, it is to develop professional police officers who understand and accept the tenets of corporateness, responsibility, and expertise and their implications for behavior and performance. Such a professional must be prepared to handle unexpected contingencies. The goal of LAPD training should be to provide its officers with the expertise to take on any contingency confidently and to maximize the chances of his resolving it successfully.

In the following example of a recruit training curriculum, we apply the recommendations from the preceding pages. The objective is to provide a demonstrative example for how the Department can revise many of its existing courses and how it might approach the design of future course offerings.

Several of the training recommendations introduced to this point that play a role in the following discussion include

- use adult learning techniques (interactive, reality-based) in curriculum development

- use problem-based learning where possible to increase retention (and to develop officer problem-solving skills)

- integrate the Department philosophy of community policing throughout curriculum

- integrate diversity awareness elements throughout curriculum

- root new material in previously learned material

- teach topics in an integrated fashion

- use scenarios for applied learning

  — emphasize verbal communications techniques in scenarios

  — add lessons learned in the field into scenarios

- make scenario debriefing a critical element of the class.

The recruit course "Use of Deadly Force" (LD 20) offers an excellent opportunity to demonstrate how the LAPD could employ the above recommendations in enhancing its Department-wide training.

The class is currently designed as a lecture. As discussed in Chapter Three, lectures are generally not the most effective teaching format for adult learners. "Use of Deadly Force" should instead be taught utilizing adult learning techniques such as problem-based learning that actively involve students. Recruits should be required to participate in and actually structure their own learning in order to increase mastery of the material. The class should be redesigned using a problem-based format, meaning that the topic is described through problems on which students work together to find solutions. This causes students to seek and uncover information relevant to the topic in the process of solving the problem. Such a challenge might involve a confrontation on skid row involving two homeless mentally ill people and a third person who is particularly prone to violent behavior. The problem should be carefully written to prompt questions and leave various courses of action open. Students would work in teams to determine the technical and communication skills they might use and identify pertinent legal and ethical issues.

Presentation of problems and scenarios is only one way an instructor might choose to teach this course. There are other techniques available for better involving students in their learning. At a minimum, the instructor should foster an open class environment in which students are free to ask for clarification or to debate issues presented. A course can incorporate active learning methods ranging from simple polling (asking students to apply their experiences or offer alternative approaches to resolving a situation), to having one speaker call on another, to more elaborate knowledge-sharing activities such as a true-false game. In the last, each student is given a card with a statement on it such as "Officer use of lethal force is justified to stop a vehicle driven at excessive speeds toward a public demonstration." The students' shared mission is to determine which statements are true and which are false, using any feasible method they desire (e.g., asking each other or looking in a resource manual). Students find the answers and solutions for themselves, learning how to use various resources that would also be of value in finding solutions to other problems in the future.

Once desired teaching methods for a course are chosen, the next step is identification of pertinent learning elements. As discussed throughout this book, an officer's professional responsibility is to serve society. Any instruction regarding the application of lethal force should therefore include community policing and cultural diversity considerations. Integrating community policing theories and cultural diversity awareness strategies throughout the deadly force curriculum is a first step toward assisting the officer in his understanding of how the three areas of use of force, community policing, and diversity awareness are inseparable during operations in the field. Instruction should incorporate other skills and knowledge likely to be called on in use-of-force scenarios, e.g., search-and-seizure procedures and arrest drills.

Certain elements will take precedence and require greater emphasis during training sessions. For LAPD officers, cultural issues are potentially a factor of significance in virtually every officer-citizen interaction. Since Los Angeles society is particularly diverse, cultural issues should be integrated throughout all relevant parts of the LAPD training curriculum. It is the responsibility of the LAPD to prepare officers to account for these differences effectively during their daily interactions with the public. Among the cultural skills and information that an instructor might include in his interactive training are

- the influence of perceptions, cultures, and prejudices on behavior

- identification of public and private agencies that provide assistance to members of the community, such as immigrants

- ways to reduce citizen complaints, lawsuits, agency-customer friction, negative media, and liability through an understanding of how situations can be perceived differently

- officer safety skills

- conflict-resolution techniques.

With community policing and diversity awareness as underpinnings for instruction, additional material can be added in a contextualized and integrated manner. Such new information is introduced in the context of existing knowledge. Use of deadly force would be incorporated into the students' knowledge base regarding other force options. That is, the instruction should be taught in the context of previously learned material and, as appropriate, prior experience. (The latter would be particularly relevant during in-service training involving long-service officers or in FTO-recruit joint training sessions.) This serves the purpose of anchoring the new learning in topics with which the student is already comfortable, thereby immediately providing context and assisting understanding. It also reminds the officer of the spectrum of tools he has available and reinforces the importance of considering all options when deciding what level of force to apply. Providing context during Department instruction improves retention and helps to prevent officers from relying on only the most recently learned techniques, regardless of their applicability. Such training not only develops expertise in applying specific skills but additionally hones communications abilities and sharpens officer judgment.

The issues inherent in use of deadly force include virtually every topic in the recruit curriculum. Connections and relationships need to be explored in the classroom and during practical exercises in the field. For instance, vehicle pull-overs, search and seizure, arrest, custody, and instruction involving persons with disabilities and special-needs populations all have ties to the topic of deadly force. An officer should be aware of the potential for a "routine" contact to escalate to a situation in which force is required in every encounter that he has with a member of the public. It is a lesson that officers need to learn early: The need for force could arise in a split second when conducting a traffic stop, taking a person into custody, or communicating with a mentally ill member of society. Integrating these and other relevant issues during training replicates the conditions the officer will confront in the field.

Developing and perfecting communication skills must likewise be a part of any deadly force instruction. LD 20 could be dramatically improved by incorporating instruction involving specific communication techniques instead of addressing them separately as is done currently in LD 3, an entirely different course. Communication skills should be fully integrated throughout LD 20 and other pertinent curricula. The force continuum cannot be taught effectively without incorporating verbal communication instruction. The concepts involved in applications of force and decisionmaking must be taught holistically. Officers need to learn how, when, and with what type of person certain communication techniques are more effective than others. This is particularly important when deadly force might be applied. A person who does not understand English or a person with a mental illness might inadvertently send aggressive signals to the officer. The officer needs to be adept at selecting from and effectively applying various modes of communication, verbal and nonverbal, under conditions of extreme stress. Partners need to know how to best assist those with whom they work to protect both fellow officers and members of the public. So taught, law enforcement personnel will gain a better understanding of how to resolve situations with the minimal force necessary.

Scenarios and other teaching tools can be designed once the curriculum content is established. Scenario training portrays the realities of policing much more closely and comprehensively than does use of the traditional lecture format. Problem-solving abilities developed through well-designed problem-based scenario training better prepare the officer for the unexpected. No number of training scenarios can cover every eventuality an officer might confront in the field. The more realistic the training and the better the understanding that the officer holds of the nature of his job, however, the more prepared he is to improvise in the inevitable unanticipated situation.

Scenarios can also enhance training approaches other than those specifically designed as "scenario based." Regardless of use, scenarios and accompanying debriefings have to be carefully constructed. They must be as realistic as possible if they are to best stimulate active student participation. When feasible, they should incorporate lessons learned taken from observations in the field. Scenarios help prepare students for the inherent complexity of police work. Department philosophies such as community policing can be integrated with diversity and special-needs issues. Information previously learned appears together with new information to expand understanding of both. The well-conceived scenario also allows officers to practice verbal communication skills as they attempt to deescalate and peacefully resolve combatant situations. Scenarios also provide officers an opportunity to practice their technical skills and consider alternatives during debriefing sessions.

The critical partner to the scenario—the debriefing—allows students to deconstruct what transpired so that they learn from their own and others' mistakes and successes. A skillful debriefing makes scenario training a more useful instruction tool. The instructor must be prepared to discuss both areas needing improvement and those in which demonstrated performance should be sustained. Each debriefing should reference the learning elements used to build the curriculum. In most adult and active learning techniques, the instructor takes on more of the role of facilitator than of expert. This is only in part true during the conduct of debriefings. The instructor facilitates the debriefing discussion and may use open-ended, nonjudgmental techniques to generate discussion. In a facilitated meeting, the group usually arrives at an answer together, one that is subjective and right for that group on that day. However, in the classroom an instructor does not leave the solution solely to the students. There are still right and wrong answers. The instructor makes sure that the class addresses critical learning points, clears up any misunderstandings, and ensures that students come up with a solution that is legal, ethical, moral, and suitable for LAPD officers.

The objective of such instruction is expert police officers—expert in technical skills applications, in communicating effectively with the public verbally and otherwise, and in making correct decisions under pressure. It is a police force in which partners know their role in best serving the interests of colleagues and the public via supporting fellow officers or intervening when a situation pushes emotions to the extreme. The objective is an expertise that by its very nature incorporates the police professional's sense of responsibility to the public and his understanding of duties to police himself as well as society.

Chapter Six

CONCLUSION

Our study of the Los Angeles Police Department training system revealed many areas in need of improvement before the LAPD can consider its officers proficient in use of force, search and seizure, arrest procedures, community policing, and diversity awareness. These findings and accompanying recommendations appear throughout the preceding pages. The recommendations are provided separately in Appendix M.

Yet there is much to be optimistic about for the leaders of the LAPD, in general, and those responsible for training, in particular. Needed improvements are rarely a function of *what* needs to be covered by the Department's curricula. Rather, the issue is one of *how* the requisite material should receive coverage. Curricula content, guided by previous studies, POST specifications, state regulation, and other guidelines, is more likely to suffer from an overabundance of guidance than insufficient direction when it comes to the five areas of interest. What is lacking is synchronization in training that brings instruction in use of force, search and seizure, arrest procedures, community policing, and diversity awareness together in ways that replicate field conditions. We found few problems with the content of recruit and continuing education courses, but the artificial manner of presenting the material actively works against understanding how the five topic areas are interrelated in day-to-day operations. The appropriate measure of success should be not the number of hours taught, but rather the effectiveness of Department officers in the field in applying the skills of concern. LAPD training has thus far failed to achieve the synchronization necessary to promote that effectiveness. What is needed is recognition that such synchronization and a means to achieve it are necessary.

There is ample evidence that the recognition is there. The consistent interaction between us and the LAPD leadership responsible for Department training has provided many opportunities to discuss the challenges and requirements confronting that leadership. All evidence points to a sincere commitment to improvement. What remains is a call for identifying a means to accomplish needed improvements. The modern concept of professionalism alone provides the synchronizing mechanism and the unifying concept needed to guide instruction in the five areas of concern and its application in the field. The overarching recommendation that the Department adopt professionalism as its guiding concept in turn spurs five primary recommendations that will facilitate this end.

OVERARCHING RECOMMENDATION

The Los Angeles Police Department should adopt a concept of police professionalism that incorporates the tenets of corporateness, responsibility, and expertise as the mechanism for guiding the development and execution of its training, to include training in the areas of use of force, search and seizure, arrest procedures, community policing, and diversity awareness.

PRIMARY RECOMMENDATIONS

- Establish an LAPD lessons-learned program.
- Introduce and maintain consistently high quality throughout every aspect of LAPD training.
- Restructure the LAPD Training Group to allow the centralization of planning; instructor qualification, evaluation, and retention; and more efficient use of resources.
- Integrate elements of community-oriented policing and diversity awareness training models throughout LAPD training.
- Develop training on use of force, search and seizure, and arrest procedures that meets current standards of excellence.

Professionalism and its tenets of corporateness, responsibility, and expertise are the foundation on which effective training can be built. The five primary recommendations provide cornerstones for that construction. Further recommendations offered herein help to shape instruction in the five areas of concern and provide direction regarding needed changes.

Mayor Hahn and Police Commission President Rick Caruso both made it clear that recommended training changes should have the least possible effects on police operations—they should take officers out of the field as little as possible.[1] We concur with this sentiment and have purposely avoided mandates of a certain number of hours of training (though primarily for other purposes) and prescriptions regarding training frequency or timing. Such recommendations are philosophically at odds with reform efforts of the LAPD, and they provide false comfort. Recommending that two hours of community policing be provided four times a year provides a convenient box for an auditor to check. It does nothing to ensure quality or retention of training covering the vital topics of concern in this study. Further, local knowledge is often the best knowledge, especially with regard to operational issues. There are training experts within LAPD who will understand this study's recommendations and can implement them in the manner that makes the most sense from the perspectives of both efficiency and effectiveness. The guidance provided in the preceding pages is explicit regarding how to enhance Department officer expertise in use of force, search and seizure, arrest procedures, community policing, and diversity awareness. Properly applied, all five areas will receive more coverage during officer instruction than is currently the case. That instruction will be more effective in teaching needed skills. Retention of the material taught will improve.

Improving training will require new resources, although perhaps less than might be thought given the considerable gains to be had through changes in approach and organizational restructuring. We understand the concerns regarding manpower and funding. To provide the LAPD with a series of recommendations that require extraordinary increases in the size of the force or exceptional funding

---

[1]Interviews with Estela Lopez.

outlays would do little other than serve as a basis for frustration. We understand that resources are limited and have therefore attempted to avoid unnecessary recommendations that require anything other than truly fundamental requirements. However, there are areas in which the LAPD will need additional sources of funding to implement recommendations and to evaluate their success. Efficient training is impossible when the training group lacks an effective automated means of managing instruction for the Department's thousands of officers. Resource management and officer time will be misused barring the introduction of an automated means of managing faculty and physical resources, schedules, officer training status, course materials, and other facets of training management. An automated learning management system will also enhance the ability of the Department to collect data that further improves training. Funds are needed for the determination of which system should be purchased, for the actual purchase of the system, and for its maintenance. The Department will also need personnel to operate such systems. The ultimate fiscal and manpower effects will depend on the systems selected and the related ability to transition positions currently focused on manual training-program management to those supporting automated management.

It is important to note that the mode of instruction that we are advocating within this book is challenging for instructors and for curriculum developers. It necessitates a considerably more intensive instructor development course, requires more up-front planning during course creation, and differs from the model that LAPD trainers have generally followed in the past. As a corollary, the process will be found to be more rewarding to many instructors. It will undoubtedly be more valuable in serving the needs of the organization if properly implemented. A professional police force requires instructors who are professionals. Those teaching must stand as examples of what the LAPD wants those learning to emulate. Currently, policies that leave instructors in teaching positions indefinitely may well be found to be counterproductive in this regard. Rotating the best officers from field duty through instructor positions brings fresh ideas into the classroom, provides the Department an opportunity to further enhance the communications and teaching skills of their best personnel via completion of an improved instructor preparation course, and gives LAPD leaders a chance to observe its rising stars as they interact with others from throughout the organization. There is a solid argument to support the conclusion that an instructor tour ought to be a reward for outstanding field performance and a prerequisite for advancement in the Department.

Our recommendations will require judgment and discretion in their application. The organization should adapt them as necessary because of the ever-changing challenges of modern law enforcement. More important than our specific individual recommendations is the need for a deliberate, general, and thoughtful shift in the philosophy of training and its purposes. Our analysis leads us to conclude that this can be done within the current constraints that influence training content.

For example, LAPD recruit training standards easily outnumber the POST minimum hours; LAPD offers nearly 200 more hours of training than POST requires.[2] None of the recommendations herein challenges the substance of external guidance. They may well question the means recommended in addressing that substance (e.g., in the case of supervision requiring a set number of hours for instruction on given topics rather than accepting that integration of such topics with other subject matter is far more effective). Points of such disagreement should be resolved with the appropriate outside agency. History reflects that most such instances are resolved in the best interests of police effectiveness and public service. In cases where external agencies fail to understand the exceptional requirements of LAPD as a department, other members of city government ought to step forward in support of their brethren. The ultimate objective is achieving what best serves the interests of the people of Los Angeles.

The first step for the Department leadership must be to adopt professionalism as fundamental to all Los Angeles Police Department activities before it can become the basis for its training. Basing instruction on the revised concept of professionalism without this commitment is pointless. Proper police performance with regard to use of force, search and seizure, arrest procedures, community policing, and diversity awareness is a function of leadership, the

---

[2]The LAPD Training Group reports this tally.

dedication of individual officers to serving society, and a training system that educates and supports those officers so that they can best perform that service. A professional force requires professional training, but no training can overcome a lack of leader support. Our interviews with Department leadership reveal a commitment to providing that support. Further, those leaders and those they lead require adequate resources from and the endorsement of other members of the city government if they are to succeed in their quest. It is only when all in their government work as a team to bring them the best in police practices that the people of Los Angeles are properly served.

PROJECT TEAM MEMBERS

RAND

Dionne Barnes-Proby is a field outreach specialist with experience in interviewing and observation. She holds a master's degree in social work, with an emphasis on cultural issues.

David W. Brannan is a political scientist at RAND with specific expertise in counterterrorism and law enforcement issues. He formerly served as a Ventura County Sheriff's deputy, where he served in many areas, including training and special weapons and tactics.

John Christian, Ph.D. student at the RAND Graduate School, was formerly a management consultant specializing in human resources and organizational effectiveness.

Scott Gerwehr is an analyst at RAND whose work focuses on the psychological dimensions of conflict, including deception, psychological operations, interpersonal and strategic persuasion, public and covert diplomacy, and recruitment/indoctrination by violent extremists.

Russell W. Glenn, Ph.D., is a senior analyst with expertise in military and police training and urban operations. His recent work includes a study on California's preparedness for a weapon of mass destruction attack, completed at the request of the state assembly.

Clifford Grammich has a Ph.D. in political science. He has helped write RAND Public Safety and Justice documents ranging from assessment of terrorism prevention measures at public facilities to evaluation of Los Angeles anticrime initiatives.

Matthew W. Lewis, Ph.D., conducts research on how technology can be applied to support learning by individuals, teams, and organizations. He has developed and fielded training/educational technology in commercial, army training, and public education settings.

Barbara R. Panitch has a master's degree in adult education and has worked with local law enforcement agencies for several years. Before working at RAND, she served as a trainer in the Seattle Police Department community policing bureau.

Elizabeth Williams, M.A., conducts field work and analysis for research projects aimed at system innovation and improvement in public safety agencies.

Consultant

Estela Lopez is a community outreach specialist. She has extensive experience in the Los Angeles community, with police-community relations, and with cultural sensitivity and training.

Expert Panel

Edmund Edelman is a former Los Angeles City Councilman and Los Angeles County Supervisor. He is a founder of the Kolts Commission on police accountability.

William Geller is a police researcher. He is an expert on issues related to use of force, community policing, and police management.

Dennis Nowicki is the former chief of police at Charlotte-Mecklenburg, N.C., and Joliet, Ill. He currently consults in managing police use of force and police discipline.

Robert Stewart is the former chief of police in Ormond Beach, Fla. He previously served with the Metropolitan D.C. Police Department. He consults on issues related to use of force and racial profiling.

Elizabeth Watson is the former chief of police for the Houston and Austin Police Departments. She now consults in the areas of community policing and police accountability.

RAND TRAINING DOCUMENT REVIEW AND CLASSROOM OBSERVATION ASSESSMENT INSTRUMENT

As of 03/27/2003

Reference # _____

Category 1. Content Analysis 2. Observation

RAND Training Document Review and Classroom Observation Assessment Instrument

* Notes: this document will be used for review of written curriculum and for classroom observation. This instrument is not intended to provide an exhaustive list of criteria on the relevant topic areas, but rather to create a 'mental set' for the reviewer.

Document Type _____	**Reviewer's Name** _____
Course Title _____	**Date Reviewed/Observed** _____
Author/Instructor _____	**Source Agency** _____
Date of Document) _____	**Related Needs/Questions** _____
_____	**Location** _____

I. GENERAL DESCRIPTION

_____

_____

II. TRAINING AUDIENCE *(check all that apply) Fill in as possible. If unknown, check with LAPD*

P1 ☐   P II ☐   PIII ☐   Investigators (DI) ☐   Supervisors (Sgt I, IIs DII, DIII) ☐   Mid Managers (Lts.) ☐   Managers (Capts. +) ☐   Civilian or other ☐

III. TRAINING FORMAT *Fill in as possible. If unknown, check with LAPD.*

Entry Level ☐   Promotional ☐   Recurrent ☐   Specialized Assignment ☐   Specialized Training (eg CNT, MFF) ☐   Roll Call ☐   Field Training ☐   Other ☐ ____

IV. TRAINING DELIVERERS (check all that apply) *Fill in as possible. If unknown, check with LAPD.*

Full- time assignment ☐   Guest speakers from community ☐   SMEs based on special assignment ☐   Team taught ☐

V. TRAINING METHODS (Check Y=Yes, N=No)

A. Administration:

	Y	N
1. Is curriculum in the new LAPD standardized format?		
2. Has the curriculum been updated within the past year?		
3. Is there a sign-off process for curriculum approval?		

B. Integration:

	Y	N
4. Is the training objective focused on participant learning for the: individual?		
organization?		
unit/team?		

C. Delivery Methods (check all that apply):

	Y	N
5. Anecdotes/examples given		
6. Case Study/scenario		
7. Demonstration		
8. Facilitation		
9. Learning Activity		
10. Lecture		
11. Panel Discussion		
12. Power point presentation as outline only		
13. Power point presentation that is interactive		
14. Problem based (begin session with researching a problem)		
15. Questions and Answers		

RAND Assessment Instrument		Page 2

	Y	N
16. Repetitive Drill		
17. Role Playing		
18. Self Paced		
19. Simulator Training		
20. Table Top (simulation/vignette)		
21. Video		
22. Workbook		
23. Are questioning techniques used?		
24. Are there explicit 'checks for understanding'?		

D. Testing Methods: (check all that apply);	Y	N
25. Quiz		
26. Multiple choice		
27. Scenario		
28. Exercise		

Additional Notes/Comments:

PLEASE MAKE A MENTAL REFERENCE TO THIS PARAGRAPH WHEN COMPLETING THE REMAINDER OF THE INSTRUMENT:

Consent Decree Paragraph 133: Within 18 months of the effective date of this Agreement, the Department shall audit police officer and supervisory officer training, using independent consultants who have substantial experience in the area of police training. The audit shall assess: ways in which LAPD training could be improved (i) to reduce incidents of excessive use of force, false arrests, and illegal searches and seizures and (ii) by making greater use of community-oriented policing training models that take into account factors including paragraph 117(c): 'cultural diversity, which shall include training on interactions with persons different races, ethnicities, religious groups, sexual orientations, persons of the opposite sex, and persons with disabilities, and also community

VI. COGNITIVE ATTAINMENT/BEHAVIOR (Check Y=Yes or N=No)

	Y	N	Comments
29. *Are officers taught not to take interactions personally?*			
30. *Is the officer taught his/her responsibility as a partner?*			
31. *Is the officer taught his/her reporting responsibility? ?*			
32. *Is the officer taught what the penalties are for committing offense?*			
33. *Is the officer taught the penalties for not reporting his/her or others actions?*			
34. *Are officers taught how to plan and coordinate individual response to incident?*			
35. *Are officers taught how to plan and coordinate team (partner) response to incident?*			
36. *Are the physical and emotional reactions of an officer to an incident addressed?*			
37. *Is the officer encouraged to tailor his/her approach to each situation (within legal, policy and ethical bounds—reviewer should comment on each area)?*			

38. *Is the officer taught what <u>not</u> to do in a particular incident?*

Additional Notes/Comments:

VII. ATTITUDE/ORGANIZATIONAL CULTURE (Check Y=Yes or N=No)

	Y	N	Comments
39. *Mission and core values of Dept stated?*			
40. *Mission and core values of Dept incorporated throughout curriculum?*			
41. *Are Dept policies stated?*			
42. *Is the chain of command described? Are individual responsibilities made clear? (i.e. are the responsibilities at different levels of chain clear? do people know what they are supposed to do?)*			
43. *Are managerial responsibilities made clear?*			

Additional Notes/Comments:

VIII. GENERAL CURRICULUM CONTENT (Complete General and at least one Topic specific sections)
(Check Y=Yes or N=No)

	Y	N	Comments:
44. *Are current legal standards included?*			
45. *Are community expectations explicitly stated?*			
46. *If Yes to previous question, is curriculum consistent with stated expectations?*			
47. *Are officers encouraged to understand nuances of the different communities on their patrol?*			
48. *Are training objectives explicitly stated?*			
49. *If Yes to previous question, does curriculum reflect these?*			
50. *Is the tactical context addressed?*			
51. *Is an understanding of implications of different cultural backgrounds conveyed? (i.e. how and when to use force?, when not to use force?, differential cultural responses to authority/arrest, etc.)*			
52. *Are diversity awareness elements incorporated in training?*			
53. *Are ethical considerations included?*			

Additional Notes/Comments:

RAND Assessment Instrument	Page 4

IX. SPECIFIC USE OF FORCE CONTENT (Check Y=Yes or N=No)

	Y	N	Comments:
54. Is "Reasonable Officer" legal standard covered?			
55. Is there a clear definition of excessive force?			
56. Are there techniques for assessing and handling resistant suspects? (i.e. "force factor, de-escalation tactics)			
57. Are there techniques for assessing and handling excessively forceful colleagues?			
58. Are reporting procedures for interactions with all suspects made clear (whether or not physical force was used)			
59. Are supervisor and manager responsibilities made clear?			
60. Is there a system for assessing and judging police behavior? Note: this may be more relevant to upper-level training.			

Additional Notes/Comments:

X. SPECIFIC - ARREST ISSUES (Check Y=Yes or N=No)

	Y	N	Comments
61. Is false arrest defined?			
62. Are the elements of crime for appropriate covered?			
63. Is "probable cause" defined?			
64. Is "reasonable restraint" defined?			
65. Are Miranda laws covered?			
66. Are detention rules covered?			
67. Warrant vs. warrantless arrests?			
68. Communication & coordination among officers when multiple officers are on scene			
69. Clarity of incident command when multiple officers and supervisors are on scene			
70. Bystander/crowd control during arrests—how & when to use (and not use) observers to facilitate successful arrests, to minimize need for force, and to reduce likelihood of complaints			

Additional Notes/Comments:

XI. SPECIFIC SEARCH AND SEIZURE CONTENT (Check Y=Yes or N=No)

	Y	N	Comments:
71. *Are legal and illegal searches and seizures defined?*			
72. *Are "probable cause" or "reasonable suspicion" defined? (i.e. PC to detain, RS to arrest)*			
73. *Are warrantless search policies covered?*			
74. *Are warrant search policies covered?*			
75. *Is acquisition of search consents (non-coercive) and various types of consents (i.e. oral, written, second-party) covered?*			
76. *Are detention policies covered?*			
77. *Is it noted that these are 4th and 14th Amendment issues?*			

Additional Notes/Comments:

XII. SPECIFIC - CULTURAL DIVERSITY (Check Y=Yes or N=No)

	Y	N	Comments:
78. *Are suggestions made for how to establish communication with different groups?*			
79. *Is there discussion of possible individual cultural biases?*			
80. *Is pedestrian and traffic stop training and data collection covered?*			
81. *Is "profiling" differentiated from "reasonable suspicion"?*			
82. *Is ethics, conflict resolution, and decision-making training included?*			
83. *Are gender equity issues inside (wrt employees) Dept addressed?*			
84. *Are gender equity issues outside (wrt citizens) Dept addressed?*			
85. *Is sexual orientation addressed?*			
86. *Are issues of racial/ethnic diversity addressed?*			
87. *Are issues of special populations addressed (physical disabilities)?*			
88. *Are issues of special populations addressed (deaf)?*			
89. *Are issues of special populations addressed (blind)?*			
90. *Are issues of special populations addressed (mentally ill)?*			

Additional Notes/Comments:

XIII. SPECIFIC - COMMUNITY POLICING (Check Y=Yes or N=No)

	Y	N	Comments:
91. Are LAPD community policing elements defined? (i.e. territorial imperative, community partnerships, marshalling resources, problem solving)			
92. Is a decision-making model presented? (i.e. problem solving or other decision making model)			
93. Does training link problem-solving methods used to address crime, disorder and fear with problem solving relevant to use-of-force control?			
94. Are crisis intervention strategies/victimology issues presented? (i.e. how to work with victims)			
95. Differential training for supervisors/managers (eg Leadership)?			
96. Is the officer taught how to determine what the community wants/needs from the police?			
97. How is the role of the officer described?			
98. Are critical thinking skills mentioned?			
99. Is supervisor leadership emphasized? Are skills presented for supervising problem solving?			

Additional Notes/Comments:

INDIVIDUAL INTERVIEW RESPONDENTS

We conducted individual interviews with the following:

- James K. Hahn, Mayor of Los Angeles

- Cindy Miscikowski, Public Safety Chair, Los Angeles City Council

- William J. Bratton, Chief of Police, Los Angeles Police Department

- Constance Rice, The Advancement Project

- Erwin Chemerinsky, University of Southern California Law School

- Merrick Bobb, Police Assessment Resource Center

- Joan Sweeney, police education consultant

- Assistant Chief George Gascón

- Assistant Chief James McDonnell

- Sergio Diaz, Captain, Training Division, and Acting Commander, Training Group

- Robin Greene, Director, Training Group

- William Sutton, Captain, Continuing Education Division

- William Murphy, Lieutenant, Continuing Education Division

- Mark Olvera, Lieutenant, Training Division.

We also conducted individual interviews with representatives of

- Police Protective League
- Command Officers Association
- Inspector General
- Police Commission
- Museum of Tolerance
- Pat Brown Institute
- ACLU
- the Hispanic community
- the Asian community.

Focus groups were conducted with LAPD personnel:

- Training group lieutenants and sergeants
- Training coordinators
- Senior lead officers
- Field training officers
- Probationers.

INDIVIDUAL INTERVIEW INSTRUMENT

RAND Interview Instrument

INTRODUCTION

RAND is a non-profit, non-partisan research organization. For this project, RAND is serving as an independent consultant working with the LAPD to enhance their training programs to help the Department better serve the community. We are looking specifically at training modules concerning use of force, laws of arrest, search and seizure, community policing, and diversity. In addition to a review of written training materials, classroom observation, and case studies, we are conducting interviews of individuals like you who have experience and/or a role vis-à-vis these LAPD training elements.

In this interview, I am going to be asking you questions about your thoughts on LAPD training in the areas I just listed. Your answers will be anonymous unless you give permission to attribute comments to you. In that case, you will be asked to sign a release form. This interview will take about 30 minutes. Thank you for your time and thoughts.

FOR REFERENCE PURPOSES ONLY!

CONSTITUENT GROUPS

This list serves to indicate the nature and type of people that we will interview. Due to time and budget constraints, we will not interview everyone on this list. We will conduct in-person (or phone) interviews with primary individuals; and will convert the questionnaire to email format for broader use. Further, we will attempt to interview of diverse cross-section of individuals in terms of demographic characteristics.

Los Angeles Police Department
    Trainers (and FTOs)
    Training Group staff
    LAPD staff (officer through command level)
    Civilians
Law Enforcement
    Federal
    California (other agencies, CHP, POST)
    Local police agencies outside of California
Los Angeles stakeholders
    Elected officials and staff
    Community representatives
    Consultants/experts (e.g., Museum of Tolerance, Pat Brown Institute, USC)
    Social Service providers
    Victims/Arrestees
Legal representatives
    City Attorney
    Defense representatives
    Legal Aid
    Legal experts (e.g., Ed Chemerinksy, Constance Rice)
Diversity/Civil Liberties Groups
    Gender
    Sexual Orientation
    Nationality
    Race
    Religion
    Physical or Mental Disability
Other
    Media
    National subject matter experts

RAND Interview Instrument   2

Interviewer's Name _____
Date of Interview _____
Interviewee's Name _____
Interviewee's
Position and Agency _____
Other _____

QUESTIONNAIRE

We have several general areas we are examining in this study. These are: use of force, laws of arrest, search and seizure, community policing, and diversity. For the best use of our time today, please feel free to focus on the areas where you feel you have the most to contribute. Please skip the areas that aren't applicable to your experience.

1) *Please briefly describe your history/experience with LAPD training.* **Prompt:** *How long have you been involved with LAPD? (2-3 min)*

2) *First, let's talk a little about training methods (5 min)*

    a) What is your opinion of the adequacy and effectiveness of the current training methods and delivery?

b) Do you think there are areas that need improvement? If so, what areas? Why?

3) *We're also interested in how officers learn their roles and are acculturated to the Department. (5 min)*

a) How do you see officers being acculturated to the Department?

b) Specifically, how are officers taught to think of their roles as authority figures?

RAND Interview Instrument   4

   c) What is the sergeant's role in officer professional development?

4) *Now we'd like to address curriculum content. (7 – 9 min)*

   a) How are the mission and core values of the Department integrated into the training materials?

   b) How often is the curriculum updated with current local, state, and federal legal standards and department policies? **If not apparent**, what is the process for updating the curriculum with current policies and standards? Is there an auditing system that ensure that training materials are consistent with training policies?

RAND Interview Instrument   5

c) Are community expectations solicited? **If so**, how? Are training guidelines adjusted to incorporate these?

d) Are issues of diversity integrated throughout training or in segmented modules? **Please cite examples**.

e) Does training address ethical decision-making issues? **If so**, how?

RAND Interview Instrument 6

f) Are officers taught what **NOT** to do? **Please cite examples** (if time permits)

g) After an incident, in addition to explaining what an officer did wrong, how does the Dept communicate to that officer and others what they Should do the next time? E.g., how are lessons learned transmitted?

h) In your opinion, is Field Training consistent with recruit training?

5) *In this study, we are looking at five specific curriculum elements: (5 min)*
    Use of Force
    False Arrest
    Search and Seizure
    Diversity (race, religion, gender, sexual orientation, physical or mental disability)
    Community Policing
    a) Drawing on your past experiences and possibly discussions that you've had, are there any particularly good 'lessons learned' or areas of concern in these areas?

    b) What trends do you see that will affect these areas of training? These can be within or outside of the Department.

6) *How do Department infrastructure systems relate to training goals? For instance, are promotion and disciplinary systems designed to be supportive of training goals (with regard to UOF, CP, etc.) (2-3 min)*

RAND Interview Instrument 8

7) *Do you find that political correctness or sensitivity considerations act as a barrier to effective teaching and understanding? (2 min)*

8) *Finally, do you have other individuals who you think would be particularly valuable to interview on these topics? (1min)*

Interviewer leave behind business card with email address.

LOS ANGELES POLICE DEPARTMENT CORE VALUES[1]

SERVICE TO OUR COMMUNITIES

We are dedicated to enhancing public safety and reducing the fear and the incidence of crime. People in our communities are our most important customers. Our motto "to protect and to serve" is not just a slogan—it is our way of life. We will work in partnership with the people in our communities and do our best, within the law, to solve community problems that affect public safety. We value the great diversity of people in both our residential and business communities and serve all with equal dedication.

REVERENCE FOR THE LAW

We have been given the honor and privilege of enforcing the law. We must always exercise integrity in the use of the power and authority that have been given to us by the people. Our personal and professional behavior should be a model for all to follow. We will obey and support the letter and the spirit of the law.

COMMITMENT TO LEADERSHIP

We believe the Los Angeles Police Department should be a leader in law enforcement. We also believe that each individual needs to be a leader in his or her area of responsibility. Making sure that our val-

---

[1]This appendix comes from LAPD, 2003e.

ues become part of our day-to-day work life is our mandate. We must each work to ensure that our co-workers, our professional colleagues and our communities have the highest respect for the Los Angeles Police Department.

INTEGRITY IN ALL WE SAY AND DO

Integrity is our standard. We are proud of our profession and will conduct ourselves in a manner that merits the respect of all people. We will demonstrate honest, ethical behavior in all our interactions. Our actions will match our words. We must have the courage to stand up for our beliefs and do what is right. Throughout the ranks, the Los Angeles Police Department has a long history of integrity and freedom from corruption. Upholding this proud tradition is a challenge we must all continue to meet.

RESPECT FOR PEOPLE

Working with the Los Angeles Police Department should be challenging and rewarding. Our people are our most important resource. We can best serve the many and varied needs of our communities by empowering our employees to fulfill their responsibilities with knowledge, authority and appropriate discretion. We encourage our people to submit ideas, we listen to their suggestions, and we help them develop to their maximum potential. We believe in treating all people with respect and dignity: we show concern and empathy for the victims of crime and treat violators of the law with fairness and dignity. By demonstrating respect for others, we will earn respect for the Los Angeles Police Department.

QUALITY THROUGH CONTINUOUS IMPROVEMENT

We will strive to achieve the highest level of quality in all aspects of our work. We can never be satisfied with the "status quo." We must aim for continuous improvement in serving the people in our communities. We value innovation and support creativity. We realize that constant change is a way of life in a dynamic city like Los Angeles, and we dedicate ourselves to proactively seeking new and better ways to serve.

LOS ANGELES POLICE DEPARTMENT MANAGEMENT PRINCIPLES[1]

1. REVERENCE FOR THE LAW

The main thrust of a peace officer's duties consists of an attempt to enforce the law. In our application of the law, we must do it within a legal spirit which was so clearly set forth by the framers of the Bill of Rights, an original part of our Constitution. That bill had as its purpose elevating the rights of each citizen to a position co-equal with the state which might accuse him. Its purpose was to provide for an enforcement of the law with fundamental fairness and equity. Because of the Bill of Rights, the dignity of the individual person in America was placed in an almost sacred position of importance.

A peace officer's enforcement should not be done in grudging adherence to the legal rights of the accused, but in a sincere spirit of seeking that every accused person is given all of his rights as far as it is within the powers of the police.

In the discharge of our enforcement of criminal statutes, the peace officer must scrupulously avoid any conduct which would make him a violator of the law. The solution of a crime, or the arrest of a lawbreaker, can never justify the peace officer committing a felony as an expedient for the enforcement of the law.

---

[1]This appendix comes from LAPD, 2003c.

We peace officers should do our utmost to foster a reverence for the law. We can start best by displaying a reverence for the legal rights of our fellow citizens and a reverence for the law itself.

2. CRIME PREVENTION TOP PRIORITY

The basic mission for which the police exist is to prevent crime and disorder as an alternative to repression by military force and severity of legal punishment. When the police fail to prevent crime, it becomes important to apprehend the person responsible for the crime and gather all evidence that might be used in a subsequent trial.

3. PUBLIC APPROBATION OF POLICE

The ability of the police to perform their duties is dependent upon public approval of police existence, actions, behavior, and the ability of the police to secure and maintain public respect.

4. VOLUNTARY LAW OBSERVANCE

The police must secure the willing cooperation of the public in voluntary observance of the law in order to be able to secure and maintain the respect and approval of the public.

5. PUBLIC COOPERATION

The degree of public cooperation that can be secured diminishes, proportionately, the necessity for the use of physical force and compulsion in achieving police objectives.

6. IMPARTIAL FRIENDLY ENFORCEMENT

The police seek and preserve public favor, not by catering to public opinion, but by constantly demonstrating absolutely impartial service to the law without regard to the justice or injustice of the substance of individual laws; by readily offering individual service and friendship to all members of society without regard to their race or social standing; by the ready exercise of courtesy and friendly good humor; and by readily offering individual sacrifice in protecting and preserving life.

7. MINIMUM USE OF FORCE

The police should use physical force to the extent necessary to secure observance of the law or to restore order when the exercise of persuasion, advice, and warning is found to be insufficient to achieve police objectives; and police should use only the reasonable amount of physical force which is necessary on any particular occasion for achieving a police objective.

8. PUBLIC ARE THE POLICE

The police at all times should maintain a relationship with the public that gives reality to the historic tradition that the police are the public and that the public are the police; the police are the only members of the public who are paid to give full-time attention to duties which are incumbent on every citizen in the interest of community welfare.

9. LIMIT OF POLICE POWER

The police should always direct their actions strictly toward their functions and never appear to usurp the powers of the judiciary by avenging individuals or the state, or authoritatively judging guilt or punishing the guilty.

10. TEST OF POLICE EFFECTIVENESS

The test of police effectiveness is the absence of crime and the presence of public order. It is not the evidence of police action in dealing with crime and disorder.

11. PEOPLE WORKING WITH POLICE

The task of crime prevention cannot be accomplished by the police alone. This task necessarily requires the willing cooperation of both the police and the public working together toward a common goal.

12. PEOPLE WORKING WITH PEOPLE

Since the police cannot be expected to be on every residential or business block, every hour of the day, a process must be developed whereby each person becomes concerned with the welfare and safety of his neighborhood. When people are working with other people in their neighborhood, they can effectively reduce crime.

13. MANAGERS WORKING WITH POLICE

Only line police officers perform the tasks for which police were created. They are the operating professionals. Supervisors and managers exist to define problems, to establish objectives, and to assist line police officers in the accomplishment of the police mission.

The evaluation of a manager should be based on the improvement and excellence of his subordinates in the achievement of organizational goals. The life's blood of good management is a thoroughly systematic, two-way circulation of information, feelings, and perceptions throughout the organization.

14. POLICE WORKING WITH POLICE

For many reasons, some specialization of work is necessary. Specialization should be created only when vitally necessary. When specialization is created, organization should be adjusted to ensure that the specialists and generalists who serve the same citizens work closely together on the common problems in as informal an organizational structure as possible. This will tend to ensure a unity of effort, resources, and the effective service to a common goal.

15. POLICE WORKING WITH CRIMINAL JUSTICE SYSTEM

It must be recognized that the police and the people alone cannot successfully resolve the problems of crime. The criminal justice system as a whole, in order to properly serve the public, must operate as a total system with all of its various elements working together. The close cooperation of the police with prosecutors, courts, and correctional officers is necessary in order to ensure the development of a safer community.

16. POLICE/PRESS RELATIONSHIPS

One of the first and most fundamental considerations of this nation's founders in drafting the Bill of Rights was to provide for a free press as an essential element of the First Amendment to the Constitution. They recognized that a well-informed citizenry is vital to the effective functioning of a democracy. Police operations profoundly affect the public and therefore arouse substantial public interest. Likewise, public interest and public cooperation bear significantly on the successful accomplishment of any police mission. The police should make every reasonable effort to serve the needs of the media in informing the public about crime and other police problems. This should be done with an attitude of openness and frankness whenever possible. The media should have access to personnel, at the lowest level in a Department, who are fully informed about the subject of a press inquiry. The media should be told all that can be told that will not impinge on a person's right to a fair trail, seriously impede a criminal investigation, imperil a human life, or seriously endanger the security of the people. In such cases, the minimum information should be given which will not impinge on the four areas and we should merely state that nothing more can be said.

In all other matters in our relationship with the media in dealing with current news, every member of the Department should make every reasonable effort consistent with accomplishing the police task in providing the media representatives with full and accurate material.

17. MANAGEMENT BY OBJECTIVES

In order to effectively deal with the most important problems, objectives must be established. The establishment of objectives and the means used to ensure that they are reached must include the participation of those involved in the task. The setting of an objective has very little meaning without the participation of those involved.

18. MANAGEMENT BY PARTICIPATION

Since employees are greatly influenced by decisions that are made and objectives that are established, it is important for them to be able to provide input into the methods utilized to reach these decisions.

Employees should be encouraged to make recommendations which might lead to an improvement in the delivery of police services and assist in the furtherance of the Department meeting its objective.

19. TERRITORIAL IMPERATIVE

Police work is one of the most personal of all personal services. It deals with human beings in life and death situations. The police officers and the people they serve must be as close as possible, and where possible must know one another. Such closeness can generate the police-citizen cooperation necessary for the involvement of the whole community in community protection. Organization of assignments should ensure that the police and the same citizens have an opportunity to continuously work for the protection of a specific community. Strength through interacting together and working together on common problems can be enhanced through officers and the people feeling at home with one another in an atmosphere of mutual cooperation. This may be described as a utilization of the "Territorial Imperative."

20. OPENNESS AND HONESTY

For police-public cooperation, there must be respect of the police by the public. This is best ensured by optimum openness of the Department in its operations. A general feeling and reality of openness must pervade the police organization. Above all, the police officer must be consistently open, honest, and trustful in all matters. A combination of honesty and openness will effectively develop respect in the community for the police and make it possible for citizens to come to them with problems and information. Where this trust does not exist because of a lack of honesty or openness, the channels of communication between the police and the public are clogged and the police must desperately struggle on alone.

LAPD ORGANIZATION CHARTS

Figure G. 1 shows the current LAPD training organization structure. Figures G.2 and G.3 show two alternative organization structures for LAPD training. For more details on the alternatives, see Chapter Three and Appendix H.

Current LAPD Training Organization Structure

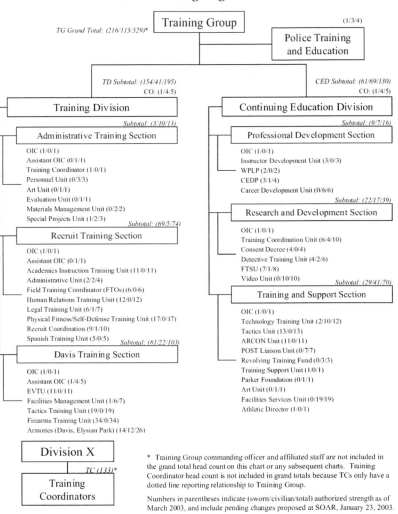

SOURCE: Robin Greene, Director of Training and Education, interview by Barbara R. Panitch, February 10, 2003.

Figure G.1

Alternative 1: Proposed LAPD Training Organization Structure

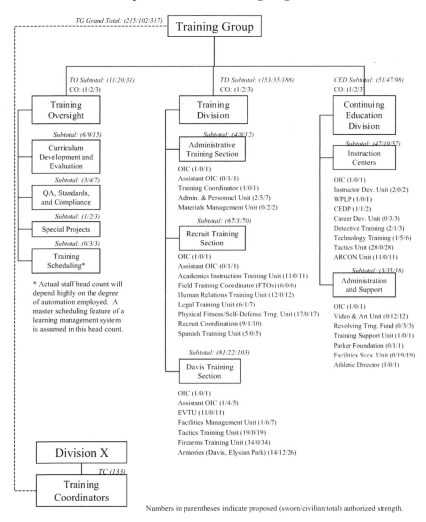

TG Grand Total: (215/102/317)

Training Group

TO Subtotal: (11/20/31)
CO: (1/2/3)

Training Oversight

Subtotal: (6/9/15)

Curriculum Development and Evaluation

Subtotal: (3/4/7)

QA, Standards, and Compliance

Subtotal: (1/2/3)

Special Projects

Subtotal: (0/3/3)

Training Scheduling*

* Actual staff head count will depend highly on the degree of automation employed. A master scheduling feature of a learning management system is assumed in this head count.

TD Subtotal: (153/35/188)
CO: (1/2/3)

Training Division

Subtotal: (4/8/12)

Administrative Training Section

OIC (1/0/1)
Assistant OIC (0/1/1)
Training Coordinator (1/0/1)
Admin. & Personnel Unit (2/5/7)
Materials Management Unit (0/2/2)

Subtotal: (67/3/70)

Recruit Training Section

OIC (1/0/1)
Assistant OIC (0/1/1)
Academics Instruction Training Unit (11/0/11)
Field Training Coordinator (FTOs) (6/0/6)
Human Relations Training Unit (12/0/12)
Legal Training Unit (6/1/7)
Physical Fitness/Self-Defense Trng. Unit (17/0/17)
Recruit Coordination (9/1/10)
Spanish Training Unit (5/0/5)

Subtotal: (81/22/103)

Davis Training Section

OIC (1/0/1)
Assistant OIC (1/4/5)
EVTU (11/0/11)
Facilities Management Unit (1/6/7)
Tactics Training Unit (19/0/19)
Firearms Training Unit (34/0/34)
Armories (Davis, Elysian Park) (14/12/26)

CED Subtotal: (51/47/98)
CO: (1/2/3)

Continuing Education Division

Subtotal: (47/10/57)

Instruction Centers

OIC (1/0/1)
Instructor Dev. Unit (2/0/2)
WPLP (1/0/1)
CEDP (1/1/2)
Career Dev. Unit (0/3/3)
Detective Training (2/1/3)
Technology Training (1/5/6)
Tactics Unit (28/0/28)
ARCON Unit (11/0/11)

Subtotal: (3/35/38)

Administration and Support

OIC (1/0/1)
Video & Art Unit (0/12/12)
Revolving Trng. Fund (0/3/3)
Training Support Unit (1/0/1)
Parker Foundation (0/1/1)
Facilities Svcs. Unit (0/19/19)
Athletic Director (1/0/1)

Division X

TC (133)

Training Coordinators

Numbers in parentheses indicate proposed (sworn/civilian/total) authorized strength.

Figure G.2

Alternative 2: Proposed LAPD Training Organization Structure

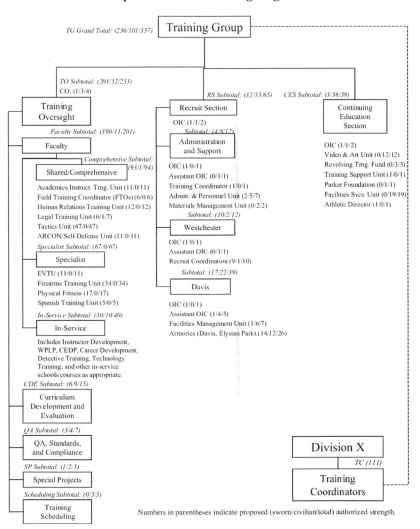

Training Group

TG Grand Total: (236/101/337)

TO Subtotal: (201/32/233)
CO: (1/3/4)

Training Oversight

Faculty Subtotal: (190/11/201)

Faculty

Comprehensive Subtotal: (93/1/94)

Shared/Comprehensive

Academics Instruct. Trng. Unit (11/0/11)
Field Training Coordinator (FTOs) (6/0/6)
Human Relations Training Unit (12/0/12)
Legal Training Unit (6/1/7)
Tactics Unit (47/0/47)
ARCON/Self-Defense Unit (11/0/11)

Specialist Subtotal: (67/0/67)

Specialist

EVTU (11/0/11)
Firearms Training Unit (34/0/34)
Physical Fitness (17/0/17)
Spanish Training Unit (5/0/5)

In-Service Subtotal: (30/10/40)

In-Service

Includes Instructor Development,
WPLP, CEDP, Career Development,
Detective Training, Technology
Training, and other in-service
schools/courses as appropriate.

CDE Subtotal: (6/9/15)

Curriculum Development and Evaluation

QA Subtotal: (3/4/7)

QA, Standards, and Compliance

SP Subtotal: (1/2/3)

Special Projects

Scheduling Subtotal: (0/3/3)

Training Scheduling

RS Subtotal: (32/33/65)

Recruit Section

OIC (1/1/2)
Subtotal: (4/8/12)

Administration and Support

OIC (1/0/1)
Assistant OIC (0/1/1)
Training Coordinator (1/0/1)
Admin. & Personnel Unit (2/5/7)
Materials Management Unit (0/2/2)
Subtotal: (10/2/12)

Westchester

OIC (1/0/1)
Assistant OIC (0/1/1)
Recruit Coordination (9/1/10)
Subtotal: (17/22/39)

Davis

OIC (1/0/1)
Assistant OIC (1/4/5)
Facilities Management Unit (1/6/7)
Armories (Davis, Elysian Park) (14/12/26)

CES Subtotal: (3/36/39)

Continuing Education Section

OIC (1/1/2)
Video & Art Unit (0/12/12)
Revolving Trng. Fund (0/3/3)
Training Support Unit (1/0/1)
Parker Foundation (0/1/1)
Facilities Svcs. Unit (0/19/19)
Athletic Director (1/0/1)

Division X

TC (111)

Training Coordinators

Numbers in parentheses indicate proposed (sworn/civilian/total) authorized strength.

Figure G.3

SUMMARY OF ORGANIZATION CHANGES

Table H.1

Alternative 1

Item	Training Group Division	Recommended Change	Net Headcount Effect
1	Training Division	Move Art Unit to new, consolidated Art & Video Unit in CED	−1
2		Move Special Projects Unit to new Training Oversight function	−3
3		Move Evaluation Unit to new Training Oversight function	−1
4		Consolidate Administrative Unit (in Recruit Training Section) with Personnel Unit (in Administrative Training Section)	0
5		Eliminate two administrative support/clerical positions in the office of the Training Division commanding officer (Alternative: eliminate two administrative support/clerical positions in the consolidated Administrative & Personnel Unit, Item 4 above)	−2
		Net Headcount Change	−7
6	Continuing Education Division (CED)	Move Instructor Development Unit to CED, Instruction Centers; eliminate one staff position as a result of synergies with Training Oversight function	−1
7		Move WPLP to CED, Instruction Centers; eliminate one staff position as a result of synergies with Training Oversight function	−1

Table H.1—continued

Item	Training Group Division	Recommended Change	Net Headcount Effect
8	Continuing Education Division (CED) continued	Move CEDP to CED, Instruction Centers; eliminate two staff positions as a result of synergies with Training Oversight function	−2
9		Move Career Development Unit to CED, Instruction Centers; eliminate three staff positions as a result of synergies with Training Oversight function	−3
10		Move Detective Training Unit to CED, Instruction Centers; eliminate three staff positions as a result of synergies with Training Oversight function	−3
11		Move Technology Training Unit to CED, Instruction Centers; eliminate six staff positions as a result of synergies with Training Oversight function	−6
12		Move Tactics Unit to CED, Instruction Centers; add 14 instructors and 1 supervisor to reduce in-service training cycle from 5 years to 2 years	+15
13		Move ARCON Unit to CED, Instruction Centers	0
14		Move one officer in charge (OIC) to new Instruction Centers Section; move one OIC to new Administration and Support Section; eliminate one OIC	−1
15		Consolidate Art Unit (in Training and Support Services Section) and Video Unit (in Research and Development Section) into new Video & Art Unit; acquire and consolidate Art Unit from Training Division	+1
16		Move Training Coordination Unit to new Training Oversight function	−10
17		Move Consent Decree Unit to new Training Oversight function	−4
18		Move FTSU to new Training Oversight function	−8
19		Move POST Liaison Unit to new Training Oversight function	−7
20		Eliminate two administrative support/clerical positions in the office of the commanding officer of CED	−2
		Net Headcount Change	−32

Table H.1—continued

Item	Training Group Division	Recommended Change	Net Headcount Effect
21	Police Training and Education	Move to new Training Oversight function, Curriculum Development and Evaluation Unit; eliminate one administrative support/clerical position	−4
		Net Headcount Change	−4
22	Training Oversight	Form Training Oversight function; add one OIC and two administrative support/clerical staff	+3
23		Form Curriculum Development and Evaluation Unit	+12
24		Form Quality Assurance, Standards, and Compliance Unit	+7
25		Form Special Projects Unit	+3
26		Form Training Scheduling Unit; actual head count will depend highly on the degree of automation employed	+3
27		Move Police Training and Education to Training Oversight function, Curriculum Development and Evaluation Unit	+3
		Net Headcount Change	+31
		Total Training Group Net Headcount Change	−12

Table H.2

Alternative 2

Item	Training Group Division	Recommended Change	Net Headcount Effect
1	Training Division	See Items 1–4, Alternative 1	–5
2		Move Academics Instruction Training Unit to new Training Oversight function, Faculty section, Shared/Comprehensive unit	–11
3		Move Field Training Coordinator Unit to new Training Oversight function, Faculty section, Shared/Comprehensive unit	–6
4		Move Human Relations Training Unit to new Training Oversight function, Faculty section, Shared/Comprehensive unit	–12
5		Move Legal Training Unit to new Training Oversight function, Faculty section, Shared/Comprehensive unit	–12
6		Move Physical Fitness/Self-Defense Training Unit to new Training Oversight function, Faculty section, Specialist unit	–17
7		Move Spanish Training Unit to new Training Oversight function, Faculty section, Specialist unit	–5
8		Move Emergency Vehicle Training Unit (EVTU) to new Training Oversight function, Faculty section, Specialist unit	–11
9		Move Tactics Training Unit to new Training Oversight function, Faculty section, Shared/Comprehensive unit; consolidate with Tactics Unit from CED	–19
10		Move Firearms Training Unit to new Training Oversight function, Faculty section, Specialist unit	–34
11		Rename Training Division "Recruit Section" and establish one OIC with one support staff	+2
		Net Headcount Change	–130

Table H.2—continued

Item	Training Group Division	Recommended Change	Net Headcount Effect
12	Continuing Education Division (CED)	Move Instructor Development Unit to new Training Oversight function, Faculty section, In-Service unit	−3
13		Move WPLP to new Training Oversight function, Faculty section, In-Service unit	−2
14		Move CEDP to new Training Oversight function, Faculty section, In-Service unit	−4
15		Move Career Development Unit to new Training Oversight function, Faculty section, In-Service unit	−6
16		Move Detective Training Unit to new Training Oversight function, Faculty section, In-Service unit	−6
17		Move Technology Training Unit to new Training Oversight function, Faculty section, In-Service unit	−12
18		Move Tactics Unit to new Training Oversight function, Faculty section, Shared/Comprehensive unit; consolidate with Tactics Unit from Training Division	−13
19		Move ARCON Unit to new Training Oversight function, Faculty section, Shared/Comprehensive unit	−11
20		Eliminate Professional Development, Research and Development, and Training and Support Sections; collapse into a single section; eliminate two OIC positions	−2
21		See Items 15–19, Alternative 1	−28
22		Eliminate four support positions for OIC	−4
23		Rename Continuing Education Division "Continuing Education Section"	0
		Net Headcount Change	−91
24	Police Training and Education	Move unit to new Training Oversight function; eliminate one administrative support/clerical position	−4
		Net Headcount Change	−4

Table H.2—continued

Item	Training Group Division	Recommended Change	Net Headcount Effect
25	Training Oversight	Form Training Oversight function; add one OIC and three administrative support/clerical staff	+4
26		See Items 23–27, Alternative 1	+28
27		Acquire faculty; see Items 2–10 and 12–19, Alternative 2	+164
28		Add 14 Tactics instructors and one supervisor to reduce training cycle time from 5 years to 2 years	+15
29		Add 22 Training Coordinators to Faculty section as full-time instructors	+22
		Net Headcount Change	+233
		Total Training Group Net Headcount Change	+8

LEARNING MANAGEMENT SYSTEMS: TOOLS TO INCREASE THE EFFECTIVENESS OF LAPD TRAINING EFFORTS

INTRODUCTION

Learning management systems (LMSs) are viewed as many things to many people. Proponents and providers tout the benefits and downplay the real challenges in integrating LMSs into the information infrastructures of organizations.[1] The goals of this appendix are to

- provide a general explanation of what LMSs are and what value they provide an organization

- describe the initial general needs of the LAPD, based on limited discussions with senior training management and staff members, then offer three very broad approaches to defining possible solutions

- enumerate a process for defining the organizational needs for learning management tools and a general approach to selecting an appropriate provider and system

- discuss the general costs associated with acquiring, implementing, and supporting an LMS

- generally help the LAPD to become an informed, demanding customer of appropriate LMS technology.

---

[1]Garvin, 1998; Moran, 2002; and Rosemann, 2002.

Each topic is addressed in turn and followed by a simple hypothetical scenario regarding how a member of the rank and file of the LAPD might use a sophisticated future LMS. The goal is to provide a brief example of the different kinds of value an LMS might provide and also to simulate thought and discussion. For example, What are other potential increases in productivity and training readiness? What are other ways to reduce human-mediated record keeping and improve the quality of training-related data?

OVERVIEW OF LEARNING MANAGEMENT SYSTEMS

LMSs and the automation they provide offer the LAPD many potential improvements to their training operations, including

- assisted training schedule development

- centralized and easily manipulated course outlines

- class lesson plans

- instructor profiles and assignment schedules

- online registration and automated course reminders

- detailed tracking of attendance and performance.

The technical definitions of LMSs vary widely. Rossett (2002), author of the American Society for Training and Development's e-learning handbook, defines an LMS as:

> Software that automates the administration of training events. The LMS registers users, tracks courses in a catalog, and records data from learners; it also provides appropriate reports to management. The database capabilities of the LMS extend to additional functions such as company management, online assessments, personalization, and other resources.

> Learning management systems administer and track both online and classroom-based learning events, as well as other training processes (these would need to be manually entered into the system for tracking purposes). An LMS is typically designed for *multiple* publishers and providers. It usually does not include its own authoring

capabilities; instead it focuses on managing courses created from a variety of other sources.

An important distinction in the definition is between the administrative information and activities surrounding training courses versus the educational content of the courses. The domain of LMSs is the administration of learning events separate from the actual teaching of courses themselves.

LMSs are widely in use by many medium-to-large, forward-thinking organizations as a way to better manage the development of the most valuable assets those organizations have: the professional capital of their workforce.[2]

GENERAL OPTIONS FOR LMSS TO IMPROVE VISIBILITY AND MANAGEMENT OF LAPD'S TRAINING EFFORTS

Based on preliminary discussions with members of the training group staff, there are both immediate and more long-term challenges to improving the visibility and management of LAPD's training efforts. Because there has been no formal needs assessment to date, this book offers only very broad options for the functionality of LMSs to improve the operations of the LAPD's training organization. The three options listed below are *not* meant to be definitive or detailed, but instead provide overviews of three different levels of functionality. Options 2 and 3 are generally supersets of the options included in lower-numbered options; Option 3 generally includes the features available in Option 1 and hence also available in Option 2. Instructor scheduling is an example: It is a feature of the minimum system (Option 1) and is therefore also a feature of full LMSs described in Options 2 and 3. The cost ranges associated with each option are also very broad. A general discussion of LMS costs also appears below.

---

[2]Schank, 2002.

Option 1: Automate Only the Process of Building a Class Schedule and Reserving Seats in Courses

Add a very basic, web-based, stand-alone course-scheduling and reservation system (one part of an LMS) to

- unburden the training management staff from hand-constructing the course schedules, room assignments, and similar primary tasks

- provide "smart" schedule-building tools to assist in avoiding scheduling overlaps, double-booking instructors, etc.

- provide web-based access to the schedules of what courses are being offered, by course, time-slot, instructor, and/or classroom

- allow students to reserve slots in courses.

Such systems

- *do not* keep any records of student performance or achievement

- *do not* include any course catalog information

- *do not* check on the qualifications or prerequisites of students reserving course seats

- *do not* link to any course content or instructor information.

General Total Cost for Option 1: In the low thousands of dollars per year for annual licenses, relatively low implementation costs in the low thousands to bring up the system and load the data (these costs are low because the option is designed to be independent of any other data system and to have absolute minimal customization), and low maintenance costs.

Option 2: Implement a Basic, Stand-Alone LMS That Does Not Integrate into Other Information Systems but Provides Many Features of Training Support

Such an LMS would include

- scheduling tools

- online catalog and information on instructors and course offerings

- online registration for students

- basic reporting of course information and student completion

- customizable reporting for management.

General Total Cost for Option 2: In the low tens-of-thousands of dollars per year for license/use fees, initial implementation costs in the low tens-of-thousands to bring up the system and load the data (more complex data loading than for Option 1, some customization, very minimal integration into other data systems) and moderate annual maintenance costs to maintain the databases.

Option 3: Implement a State-of-the-Art LMS That Integrates Seamlessly into Other Information Systems and Provides a Rich Set of Features for Training Support

A full-featured LMS adds many potentially important components to the capabilities in Option 2, above. Included are integration of the LMS into a suite of learning tools and online, distance-learning content (support for student learning and actual course materials) that is also generally included in the category of information systems called learning-content delivery systems:

- online assessments and detailed, secure student records

- student tool-kits to help them manage their training and "career-pathing" opportunities in the force, based on current and future courses to be offered

- tracking of web-based, distance-learning courses at a fine level of performance, e.g., down to the time spent per web-page and each response to a question on a quiz or test

- customizable "digital dashboards" for reporting data from the LMS for managers at all levels of the organization to allow them to manage the training process

- online collaboration tools for groups to work together, at a distance

- instructor tool-kits to allow instructors to post course materials and examination feedback, to have threaded discussions, to conduct online office hours, etc.

- learning content management systems that are repositories for all the course materials (e.g., slides, tests, graphics) and carefully controlled access to these resources

- provision of detailed archiving of all aspects of the LMS and student performance

- capabilities for students to submit their work online, to build portfolios of their best work for course evaluation and eventual inclusion in their human resources files.

General Total Cost for Option 3: In the high hundreds-of-thousands or low millions of dollars for implementation, and significant annual costs for licenses, operation, and support.

SELECTING A LEARNING MANAGEMENT SYSTEM

Selecting any significantly expensive and complex software for an organization should be done using appropriate care and established methods. There are varying suggestions in the literature for the process of selecting a learning management system.[3] The following steps are fairly general:

1. Begin the selection and implementation process with a thorough "needs analysis": What are the LAPD organizational requirements and LMS features appropriate for LAPD needs?

2. Understand the e-learning industry standards that the LMS should follow: What are current and evolving requirements so that the product chosen will function well over the next five–ten years?

3. Master the terms and acronyms associated with the industry.

4. Establish who are the current major players in the market and look for general industry/market feedback on customer satisfac-

---

[3]Hall, 2002; and Tiwana, 1999.

tion: What is the marketplace saying about their experiences with different vendors?

5. Build a comparative table to analyze key features and benefits across products.

6. Write an effective LMS request for proposal (RFP).[4]

7. Develop questions for each vendor who responds to the RFP to drill down into their proposal and clarify outstanding issues; talk with customers of each qualifying vendor to assess satisfaction with the product, service, and support provided.

In carrying out the first step of doing a "needs assessment," it is important to include all the relevant "stakeholders" in the training group who would use the LMS.[5] In the case of the LAPD, this would potentially include

- training group management staff

- training group managers themselves (people who schedule and provide logistics support of course delivery)

- training deliverers (the training group and CED instructors)

- trainees (recruits and in-service students).

If the system will be interfacing with other information systems, such as those in personnel/human resources, then the needs-assessment effort would also include other senior managers in the organization to ensure that their information/reporting needs and management goals are covered by the LMS. There may also be other offices within the LAPD that might want to take advantage of training data such as audit units or internal affairs. These should also be polled during the needs-assessment phase.

There is also the critically important task of understanding the systems integration aspects of implementing the technology within the information infrastructure of the LAPD. Will the LMS be pulling in-

---

[4]Hall (2002) offers a sample RFP at his web site as well as other resources: www. brandon-hall.com, last accessed June 20, 2003.

[5]Piskurich, 2000.

formation in an automated fashion from the other LAPD systems? Specifically, how will the LMS interface with the personnel systems and their risk-assessment systems?

There are also the more mundane questions of hardware support: On what servers will the system run? Who maintains them? Do they have the capacity to support the application? Such questions are critical to ensure that the implementation will appropriately fit the existing information architecture and provide quality service for the lifetime of the system.

As with most large-scale organizational change efforts, the up-front effort in planning and preparation ensures a much higher probability of success. Choosing an LMS is no different. Unless the LAPD chooses the first option above, selecting a simple scheduling and registration system, we strongly recommend that for any more significant effort at providing LMS capability, the LAPD should carefully consider engaging the service of a for-profit consulting group that has done several successful implementations of LMSs for similar-sized organizations. There is no substitute for experts who can guide the needs assessment, system selection, customization, and implementation. The stakes and costs are high, so having unbiased expertise on the side of the LAPD when going to the marketplace is a prudent measure.

There are many providers of LMSs in the marketplace today, Hall (2002) lists the following as significant:

- Docent
- Isopia
- Learnframe
- Saba
- TEDS
- THINQ training software.

RAND has done no research on these firms and provides no recommendations about providers.

LMS COST INFORMATION: ROUGH GUIDES FOR ESTIMATING COSTS

Like most answers to most complex questions, the unsatisfying an-swer to the question of how much LMSs cost is "It depends." Costs will vary depending on

- the number of courses you want to administer

- the number of students you will be serving

- the provider you choose

- the maintenance agreement you choose

- the different kinds of features you can add, e.g., "smart" tools to assist in avoiding scheduling overlaps or double-booking in-structors

- the amount of integration that your system will involve with ex-isting legacy systems

- the amount of sharing of data between the system and the per-sonnel systems

- the amount of historical data you want to load into the system

- the detail of the data you collect on student progress

- the amount of customization you would like to make for stan-dard managerial reports

- many other factors that a consultant could help the Department to identify during a requirements-gathering and system-design process.

In general, costs for implementing LMSs include the following cate-gories.

Implementation Costs

- Costs of searching for and hiring a firm to provide "systems inte-gration" expertise, if this is to be a major software integration ef-fort.

- Costs of a detailed needs assessment/requirements definition effort to specify the system needed.
- Costs of implementing the system
  — customization of software
  — loading initial data
  — possible computer hardware upgrade costs to support the LMS and associated databases.
- Costs for "internal marketing" of the system to raise awareness and gain acceptance.

Operational Costs

Initial and ongoing costs for training users (both end users and training administration staff).

- Annual costs for
  — software license (can vary "per seat" or other usage metrics)
  — software maintenance contract
  — part-time "systems administrator" and "database technician" roles
  — archival data storage fees.

The Ephemeral Issue of "Cost Savings"

There is a natural interest to measure cost savings when implementing moderate- to large-value software systems aimed at improving efficiencies and productivity. It has traditionally been difficult to measure cost savings of technology implementations in a systemic way. Freed-up person-hours often are retasked to other needy efforts within the organization. Cost reductions in one area are often countered by new costs in another (Zuboff, 1988), e.g., having a part-time systems administrator and database technician to maintain the system when you are replacing people who used to do the same task with paper or spreadsheets.

However, what is generally found is that the quality of service goes up from the perspective of the group being served by the new information system (Zuboff, 1988). New efficiencies appear: Officers have their training information at a single, easily accessible site. Searching for and selecting courses becomes easier. Managers can find out where their in-service officers are while in their training, at all times. These and other capabilities, such as centralized instructor scheduling, are fundamentally critical to the Department reorganization as discussed in the body of this book.

In sum, people will generally accomplish more with greater ease, but measuring the cost savings is difficult.

SUMMARY: BENEFITS WILL COME, BUT SO TOO WILL COSTS

LMSs and the automation they provide offer the LAPD many potential improvements to their training operations. As other organizations will attest (Schank, 2002), better management of the development of the professional capital of their workforce greatly improves the quality of their employees and appears to improve employee retention. This makes sense given that people will generally stay with a job if it continues to engage/challenge them intellectually and offers clear paths for learning and growth. LMSs are tools to help provide structured access to that learning.

While highly desirable from a number of perspectives, LMS automation clearly comes with considerable up-front and life-cycle costs in terms of manpower and dollars. Committing to such a system will require an initial investment of money, time, and effort to succeed, and it will need to have strong organizational support at a high level. Without significant will and senior attention, such an effort could end with an inappropriately specified system implemented badly and hence unused. From such an investment will come organizational returns in the form of efficiencies and improved effectiveness, but they will take some time to realize.

For any serious effort at providing LMS capability, we strongly recommend engaging the service of a for-profit consulting group that has done several successful implementations of LMSs for similar-sized organizations. The expertise of having experienced, unbiased talent in a "systems integrator" or "general contractor" role to guide and aid in the design of the system and the selection of a provider, and to lead the resultant system's implementation, could be invaluable.

CASE STUDIES—A BRIEF COMPENDIUM OF POLICE TRAINING INNOVATIVE PRACTICES

INTRODUCTION

This compendium reviews innovative practices of law enforcement training relevant to the topics under review in this project. Its methodology, described below, featured interviews with personnel at police organizations recognized for innovative programs and one police organization operating under a consent decree. In the interviews, we discussed issues such as identifying challenges to law enforcement training; how police leadership affects overall training; community policing; and key issues such as use of force, community relations, and training programs (including field training and training of trainers) that departments have used to deal with specific issues in their communities. Specific suggestions on how the LAPD might implement some of these innovative practices are noted near the end of this appendix.

METHODOLOGY

This review is not a comprehensive analysis of U.S. law enforcement training techniques; rather, it discusses training programs that have been effective in dealing with challenges similar to those faced by the LAPD. To select departments for analysis, we relied on RAND personnel, industry knowledge, a literature review, and the expert panel of law enforcement professionals familiar with the issues of use of force, arrest procedures, search and seizure, community policing, diversity, training, leadership, ethics, and police management. We sought departments and training facilities that

- had generally effective training programs

- had training programs that responded effectively to specific problems

- had otherwise notable training programs.

Interviews were sought with representatives of nearly two dozen police agencies, including federal law enforcement and other agencies operating under consent decrees. From these, representatives of thirteen agreed to be interviewed: Austin Police Department, Charlotte-Mecklenburg Police Department, Houston Police Department, Miami Police Department, Michigan State Police, New York City Police Department, Reno Police Department, Royal Canadian Mounted Police, San Diego Police Department, San Francisco Police Department, Seattle Police Department, Steubenville (Ohio) Police Department, and the FBI.

IDENTIFYING CHALLENGES TO LAW ENFORCEMENT TRAINING

Respondents emphasized that law enforcement cannot be static. Training must therefore be designed to fit a changing environment. Demographics, social conditions, and issues of public interest are continually changing, and training must be designed to help police deal with these changes.

Few departments had a fixed methodology ready for identifying new issues to address through training. Some interviews suggested that a good working relationship between internal affairs (or the division charged with handling citizen complaints against officers) and the training division leadership was helpful in identifying patterns in areas such as use of force or ethical questions that recur in citizen complaints.[1]

---

[1]James Lynch, Captain, San Francisco Police Department, phone interview by Dave Brannan, August 30, 2002.

The San Francisco Police Department internal affairs division, for example, uses an automated computer program to identify officers most inclined to use force in a given situation.[2] While this program is being used primarily for disciplinary purposes, it could be modified to identify training needs as well. The information is shared with the division for use in developing its curricula. Some departments' training organizations rely on committees for advice regarding needed changes in curricula or training techniques. A San Diego regional training facility, for example, uses a citizen advisory panel that forwards public views on desired changes in training. A committee of local police chiefs complements this citizen input by reviewing what changes are called for to improve training across their several departments.[3] The regional nature of this cooperative partnership allows sharing of information and resources so that departments can coordinate their training responses to emerging issues.

Using community panels for training advice assumes a relationship involving a reasonable level of trust between community leaders and their police department. To function effectively, department officials should establish an environment in which they are seen to be *responding* to community needs rather than *reacting* to complaints.[4]

LEADERSHIP AND THE IMPORTANCE OF AN INTEGRATED PHILOSOPHY

Interviewees repeatedly noted that effective training hinges on department leadership and commitment to training (in addition to the existence of adequate training resources to accomplish necessary tasks). Managers told us that training was effective only to the extent that entry-level recruits and experienced officers perceived leadership to be in support of the training. Every training leader added that on-the-job instruction from training officers, senior officers, and recognized leaders (not necessarily of higher rank) was more impor-

---

[2]Ibid.

[3]Robert Stinson, Lieutenant, San Diego Police Department, phone interview by Dave Brannan, September 3, 2002.

[4]Lynch interview, 2002. Harold Medlock, Captain, Charlotte-Mecklenburg Police Department, phone interview by Dave Brannan, August 31, 2002.

tant and ultimately more effective in training new recruits than the information given in the classroom. One training leader noted

> A change to the training philosophy can't be made without an absolute commitment on the part of the chief and his staff. We would not have been able to transform this department's method of policing if it had not been for the fact that the chief made it the matter by which you stood or fell in your career. It's a way of life now. This is just how we do things around here now. People know that if they want to go anywhere—they have to adopt the philosophy.[5]

Some interviewees stressed that few other issues are as important as ongoing integration of work and training by police leadership.[6] The basic training at the academy or other initial instructional facility is seen as a base from which on-the-job learning should start. The effectiveness of training is minimal without clear direction from the department leadership that training philosophy and techniques are important and must align with the values and ideals of the department. A "wink" or a "nod" contradicting training can be devastating to its effectiveness, whether from a FTO stating "Forget what they taught you; this is how it's done on the streets" or in the form of a senior leader failing to reflect the standards inculcated in recruits.

Command staff must support and encourage training goals in word and action. Lip service alone will never suffice to convince lower ranking officers of a command's commitment to change.[7]

COMMUNITY POLICING: MORE THAN JUST A PROGRAM

Leadership Requirements

Community policing has become a catchword for alleged forward thinking and vague forms of community partnerships. For depart-

---

[5]Medlock interview, 2002.

[6]Medlock interview, 2002. Stinson interview, 2002.

[7]Several interviewees suggested that line officers and supervisors were quick to discern between those policies the administration actually believed in and those offered primarily for public consumption.

ments that are serious about developing meaningful partnerships with the communities they serve, leadership must be clear in expressing its intent in this regard.[8]

The Royal Canadian Mounted Police (RCMP) department undertook to make significant philosophical and operational changes in its approach to policing during the 1990s. An initial step in a program of introducing community policing was to overhaul RCMP cadet training. Four foundational elements were introduced that were to underlie all aspects of RCMP preparation and subsequent service:

- mission

- vision and values of the department

- the CAPRA problem-solving model

- the incident management model (regarding the use of a "force continuum").

Subsequent to introducing the new approach, the RCMP director of training looked back and identified some of the difficulties inherent in the RCMP approach to change. His frank appraisal suggested that the RCMP may have overused the CAPRA model in the early stages. Additionally, he noted that it was difficult to sustain the energy, communication, and marketing of the message over the course of recruit training. He attributed the success finally achieved in gaining department-wide acceptance of the new program to the support provided by RCMP leadership, especially those in top management positions.[9]

Consistent leadership means staying the course, to include ensuring that an organization's operational philosophy is clear and that its meaning does not change during training. That consistency is fundamental. With it, effective training and quality leadership send the same message, a message that will be reflected in the actions and

---

[8]Two interviewees said that their department's implementation of community policing failed before it actually took hold in either the department or the communities they served.

[9]Garry Bell, Director of Cadet Training, and Joanne White, Learning and Development Center, Royal Canadian Mounted Police, phone interview by John Christian, February 25, 2003.

attitudes of officers on the street. Other organizational policies must further sustain the continuity of the message. Promotion criteria are another key in this regard. The Charlotte-Mecklenburg Police Department requires officers seeking advancement to participate in training that tests their knowledge and commitment to the department philosophy.[10] Command-level leaders are taught the core values and philosophies of community policing through problem-based learning methods.[11] This training serves as an essential element that allows leaders to effectively lead their personnel through the problem-solving process while setting an example for every subordinate's behavior.

Police Officer Training

Police officer training that attempts merely to "add on" classes on topics such as community policing and diversity will not provide the necessary integration of training, problem-solving techniques, and patrol procedures.

The agencies that seem to have the most success at operationalizing community policing in their department philosophy rely on a problem-based learning curriculum through which they use problem solving during instruction involving community policing and other components of training. They consider community policing as a fundamental underpinning of all police work. For example, use-of-force policy is considered within the context of the department's relationship with the community much as has been suggested should be the case for the LAPD in the main body of this study. Use of force is viewed as a technique that police use when other techniques are inappropriate or insufficient to protect community members, including the law enforcement officer. Other patrol procedures, such as arrest and search and seizure policies, are similarly taught from a police–community relations perspective.

The aforementioned RCMP recruit training provides a striking example of how community policing and problem solving can improve police academy instruction. The Canadians abandoned conven-

---

[10]Medlock interview, 2002.

[11]Medlock interview, 2002.

tional, lecture-based academy training in favor of an innovative, scenario-based program as part of their training revolution.[12] RCMP Director of Cadet Training Garry Bell observed

> The program is principle centered, value driven, and hinges upon a community policing philosophy. It is geared to teaching problem solving, critical thinking, proactive policing and community policing principles. What we aim to produce is a troop or an individual capable of both interdependent and independent kinds of actions, so we stress teamwork and individual responsibility throughout the program. We see our basic training program as the first step in a life-long learning process. Continuous learning is something that is drummed into the cadets right from the get-go.

> The scenarios are the center point of a whole problem-based learning format. We use real-world problems as the organizing construct around which all of the knowledge, skills and abilities are brought together in an integrated fashion. The problems are chosen to lead us into particular training issues. We use scenarios as teaching instruments, we use them as practice for skill acquisition, and we use them for testing and assessment. We rely upon scenarios, with ascending levels of complexity, throughout the program. We go from paper-based problem-solving scenarios through peer role-playing scenarios to actor-simulated role plays in full mock-detachment settings. We use scenarios because they hammer home to cadets what the bigger picture is.

Similarly, the New York Police Department finds it valuable to role-play many common police-public scenarios. Using police students as citizens, the department communicates the message that officers are servants of their community. "We make the officer know that he is not a soldier, that it's not a war on crime" cites Director of Training James Fyfe. Though operating in a changed environment since the attack on the World Trade Center on September, 11, 2001, the director of training communicates that officers are always part of the city's society. The department uses success stories to establish role models and in developing training scenarios. Department representatives informally surveyed precinct officers to learn who they would rather work with and why. They then studied those officers' behaviors to

---

[12]Bell interview, 2003.

determine the vital characteristics found in such officers. One finding was that the role-model officers are less judgmental about community members than is the average officer.

Many departments also stress the importance of self-policing and other ethical behavior. Police leaders from Austin are among those who found that inappropriate behavior is often due to a lack of field supervision. They advocate taking strong steps to be sure that middle managers are held directly responsible for officer behavior.

Community Contact and Use of Force

The San Francisco Police Department encourages a community service ethic in its entry-level trainees by taking them to community gatherings and events. The Reno Police Department requires field training program participants to develop a neighborhood portfolio detailing local resident characteristics, businesses in the area, and environmental issues that might affect community policing operations.[13] Other departments have established community and cultural awareness groups along similar lines.

San Francisco, Seattle, San Diego, and many other cities have found that running community police academies and holding meetings in the community rather than at police facilities are effective in opening lines of communication.[14] Such activities have been successful in abetting public understanding of the conditions under which police work and the constraints on what they are allowed to do. Establishing such community policing relationships virtually always suffer an initially awkward group formation phase. Perseverance has often rewarded those departments willing to work through these problems to the point of achieving a maintainable forum for police-community exchange based on open communication and trust.

---

[13]Jerry Hoover, Chief, Reno Police Department, phone interview by Dave Brannan, September 25, 2002. For a more complete description of this tool, see the field training subsection of this appendix.

[14]Community police academy is a term used by some departments to describe their ongoing education efforts for the public about policing techniques and how the community can more effectively support those efforts.

Additionally, active recruiting of police officers from communities served by a department can help achieve community policing goals.[15] Interview respondents suggested that diversity issues or those regarding race, gender, and sexual orientation are most effectively handled by actively recruiting officers from areas of the community likely to be frustrated by their exclusion.[16] It is important to note that "community" in this sense refers to a demographic segment of the public and not simply a particular geographic area within city limits.

These approaches to community policing are further seen as making officers more attuned to their communities and hence less likely to use force inappropriately.[17] The rewards of these efforts at greater community contact and melding such topics as use of force and community service sometimes have direct positive effects in the field. Several agencies and training program representatives spoke of how those involved in successful community policing programs had at times given them considerable latitude for investigating serious uses of force in neighborhoods that had traditionally been dangerous or hostile to police.[18]

The Challenging Issue of Race

The issue of race is often a source of tension, one that can underlie confrontations between police and community members. The law enforcement community is divided on how best to deal with this challenge. Representatives of several departments reported dealing with racial issues in their approach to community policing but were unable to propose consistently successful ways to broach and deal with the issues.

Racial profiling is currently a volatile topic in cities. To address this issue, the Seattle Police Department arranged a forum with police and city government representatives for clergy, business, and civil rights leaders as well as other residents of the local community. The

---

[15]The San Francisco Police Department was most emphatic on this point.

[16]Lynch interview, 2002.

[17]Stinson interview, 2002. Lynch interview, 2002.

[18]Medlock interview, 2002. Stinson interview, 2002.

meeting was chaired by a recognized personality from the community whose considerable ability, including a willingness to ask hard questions and mediate a potentially explosive environment, was crucial to the effectiveness of the meeting.

The department went beyond the norm for opening communication with the community. Police representatives tolerated sometimes very harsh criticism and were in return provided the opportunity to present their perspectives, including a belief that officers needed to be allowed to exercise *discretion* (versus *discrimination*) in their contacts with the public.[19] The department followed up this initiative with television public service announcements regarding the discussion that outlined police plans to address community concerns.

The New York Police Department has approached community representatives directly in seeking input on training and other concerns. Its director of training has access to a "visitor's committee" whose members represent many in the composite city community. The purpose of the committee is to let department leaders know what issues are brewing in the community so that they can be considered in light of how training or other resources might be employed in addressing them. Members serve on a three-year rotating basis.

Miami Police deliberately incorporate diversity issues into many types of police training. In one course, Miami has chosen to focus on each officer's awareness of his own prejudices and related problems in dealing with various demographic groups.

Field Training

The San Jose model for field training officers (the "FTOProgram") has for the past two decades been widely accepted by the law enforcement community as an example for the effective training of new officers. Recently, the Reno Police Department has revised and refined the program to reflect changing needs in its community and recent developments in adult learning. Rather than simply focusing on behavior modification as taught in the San Jose model, Reno's efforts

---

[19]Tag Gleason, Captain, Seattle Police Department, phone interview by Dave Brannan, September 5, 2002. See Seattle Police Department, 2001b.

have centered on problem-based learning techniques, including problem-oriented policing.

The Reno Police Department has changed the name of the field training program to Police Training Officer (PTO), with the intent of reflecting its true role in post-academy training. The PTO program features a unique training relationship in which trainers act more as developmental coaches than as evaluators.[20] The program has four primary areas of learning: patrol, investigations, emergencies, and nonemergency situations. Each of these four principal areas is divided into 15 core competency areas developed by the individual departments, allowing departments or their divisions to adjust the curriculum to address specific issues in their area.[21] The program provides participants with a structured problem related to real-life situations that participants might encounter in a training area.[22] The training guidance that accompanies each teaching problem identifies the learning issues that are to be covered during instruction. The structured problems allow participants to work through difficult issues and find contacts for additional expertise before assuming full patrol duties.

Reno's Approach to "Failing Forward" and Introspective Analysis

Trainees can be "coached" to think through problems by asking themselves fundamental questions and applying problem-solving principles, or by asking what is and should be known about a situation, developing a course of action, and evaluating the outcome for insights to be applied to future problems.

The student is allowed to "fail forward"—that is, to try his own way even if it is not the best way—in situations that are not life threatening or that do not compromise ethics and professionalism. Participants are asked how and why they devised their response to the

---

[20]For a complete explanation of the San Jose model as it is taught today, see Kaminsky, 2000.

[21]For a more complete description of the program, see Hoover, Cleveland, and Saville, 2001.

[22]Ibid.

problem, including the resources they used, as well as what better way they might handle a similar incident in the future. In other words, participants are held responsible for their actions while learning new ways of problem solving for the next incident.

Developing Networks During Field Training

The police training programs identified here also encourage participants to develop networks for information and expertise in a wide variety of areas from many different sources. One such source, as mentioned above, is the neighborhood portfolio several departments, including Charlotte-Mecklenburg, Reno, Austin, and Seattle, require of their new officers. In addition to the content mentioned above, neighborhood portfolios also include identification of community groups and issues, advisory boards, and other resources for advice on solving problems encountered on patrol. Officers also learn the backgrounds and skills of their fellow officers and thereby learn of colleagues who could assist on issues and challenges that they might not be able to handle on their own.[23]

Training the Trainers

Training at any level depends considerably on the quality of instructors. Those teaching and training law enforcement recruits come from various educational, personal, and professional backgrounds. A trainer teaching criminal law in the academy may have a different focus than the trainer for defensive tactics. This is appropriate, but trainers still need to share attitudes regarding the purposes of training and its integration with community policing work. The Michigan State Police department has carefully designed its training for trainers with this objective in mind.[24]

Trainers in the department are first taught the overarching department philosophy from which the educational goals are derived.[25]

---

[23]Steve Pitts, Commander, Reno Police Department, phone interview by Dave Brannan, September 25, 2002.

[24]Michigan State Police, 2001.

[25]Gene Hoekwter, Commanding Officer, Michigan State Police, phone interview by Dave Brannan, August 27, 2002.

Often-ignored vision and mission statements are emphasized throughout the training of trainers. Chosen instructors are those who willingly adhere to the vision and philosophy of the department. This careful selection helps ensure that the intensive two-week training program for instructors will inculcate in all trainers the values the department wants to emphasize in training recruits and officers.[26]

The two-week training of instructors is based on four elements of group formation: (1) forming, (2) storming, (3) norming, and (4) performing.[27] The core concept of each area is that education and discipline need to be interwoven to effectively train a recruit for professional service to the community. Recruit and trainer are bound by a defined compact emphasizing the trainer's intention to teach, and the commitment that new officers should learn and exhibit in their work the qualities they are taught. The goal of the program is to instill a commitment to professionalism and the core values of the department rather than protection of fellow officers at any cost.[28]

USING INNOVATIVE PRACTICES IN THE LAPD

It is sometimes difficult to transfer techniques that work in one city or agency to another, especially to Los Angeles, one of the most heterogeneous and fast-changing cities in the world. However, while it is true that every department operates in a unique environment with its own history, culture, and community needs, experiences elsewhere should not be dismissed simply because they come from elsewhere. These programs can be modified as appropriate for effective use in Los Angeles.

---

[26]Hoekwter interview, 2002.

[27]Michigan State Police, Training Division, 2001, pp. 9–35. In this section of the manual the point is made that their particular training philosophy rejects the traditional "boot-camp" styled para-military training and replaces it with a regimen that more closely relates to military officer training and stresses leadership and problem solving rather than simply following orders. In this regard, the manual has relied heavily on the work of James J. Fyfe.

[28]See Michigan State Police, 2001, p. 7. Hoekwter interview, 2002.

Identifying Training Challenges

The LAPD should build on its community police advisory boards, community police academies, and other efforts to continually engage the community. Experiences in Los Angeles and similar police initiatives for dealing with local communities elsewhere validate the benefits of these efforts. Such formal interactions are only one means of determining citizen concerns, however. The number of interactions Department officers will collectively have on a given day will dwarf the total number of community policing meetings held in a year. Police on the streets, those trained in, and willing to exercise their talents in, interpersonal relations will be invaluable sources of neighborhood input given that their Department has a mechanism for collecting such issues and leadership willing to listen.

Philosophy and Leadership

LAPD leadership should inculcate its officers with training and policing philosophies compatible with each other and the community it serves. Community-based policing relying on problem-based learning and emphasizing problem solving appears to be the approach achieving the best results in police organizations throughout the continent. Both adult education theory and these confirmatory cases suggest that it would be a highly effective training methodology for the LAPD.

Training to best serve the community requires broad commitments for which a department may find difficulty in gaining acceptance. Significant changes in command personnel positions were among the steps necessary to generate the leadership support needed for cultural change in other departments considered in our case study analyses.

Implementation

Departments implementing the changes needed for community police training have found success through the following sequence:

1. At the leadership and command levels of the department, there has to be total adherence to and understanding of community

policing and its principles. This requires bold leadership by the chief and his staff, supplemented by well-crafted leadership training throughout the organization.

2. Entry-level and field training programs must be altered to reflect new training goals. The recruit and in-service training cadre must share the philosophy and goals of department leadership and integrate them throughout training.

3. Promotion requirements should include training in and a demonstrated understanding of community policing.

4. Such philosophical shifts as community policing are best introduced at the division or station level to engage line supervisors and the informal leaders of the organization in the processes of training and field implementation.

Significant investments are needed for training innovations. Implementing the most effective training practices is not an overnight process. While certain innovations can be implemented without great cost in the short term, it appears that the most significant changes for LAPD training will require a long-term leadership commitment and significant investment in resources, most notably that of time.

COMMUNICATIONS VARIABLES

This appendix provides a detailed listing of various communications characteristics and circumstances in which they might be pertinent. It is not exhaustive, but rather is presented in the interest of providing officers with a list of the types of variables they can select from as they confront challenges in the field. In any given situation, the officer might select one, two, or several of these approaches during the interaction. For further discussion, refer to Chapter Five, subsubsection "The Variables in Persuasive Communications."

CATEGORY 1: SOURCE—THE POLICE OFFICER

Credibility

The more credible the source of a persuasive communication, the more likely it is to be obeyed. An officer can be a credible source for more than one reason. One is *authority:* the obvious source of establishing police officer authority is simply appearing in uniform, emerging from a patrol car, and stating "I am Officer Smith of the LAPD." However, depending upon the audience and circumstances, the use of the Department as a source of credibility or authority may actually backfire—e.g., in the case of community members historically victimized by LAPD officers. An alternative may be for the officer to quickly establish historical ties to the community, e.g., "I'm Officer Smith and I grew up three streets from here on Main." The important point is that credibility and authority can spring from more than one source and that officers exert some control over this variable.

CATEGORY 2: SUBJECTS—MEMBERS OF THE PUBLIC

Culture

Different cultural backgrounds shape our perceptions of the world in strikingly different ways. An individual whose family has recently immigrated after fleeing persecution by an authoritarian regime is likely to view police with suspicion and fear. The "command presence" that might gain voluntary compliance from an individual of one culture can induce hostility and aggression in someone from another. Officers would be well served were their training to provide them prior knowledge of the cultural norms of audiences with which they are likely to interact. Moreover, a few simple questions might elicit helpful information in determining how to best communicate with an individual. The answers could be critical in establishing the proper choices of language, tone, and other behavioral elements.

Idiom

Language choice—in all of its particulars—can play a pivotal role in any interaction. Disrespectful, hostile, domineering language is an obvious candidate for eliciting belligerent reactions, but so is simply choosing the wrong word at the wrong time or mistranslating a foreign language. Officers should be aware of the varieties of languages spoken in their areas of operations and be practiced in switching linguistic gears. Assigning officers familiar with a language (and other forms of communications) to communities that take advantage of that ability can have significant payoffs. It is important, however, that the multilingual officer know the language not only as it is taught in schools but also as it is used on the streets that he and his fellow officers patrol.

Existing Opinions and Attitudes

Related to—but distinct from—culture are opinions and attitudes. There is likely a broad spectrum of attitudes regarding police officers, police tactics, police brutality, and the utility of community policing within a given culture. An individual officer should therefore not prejudge an individual's views based on culture, race, or other demographic characteristic. Prejudice is a bane to good communications and can significantly increase risk to officers in any circumstances. An alternative to prejudice is inquiry. Training should seek to make officers comfortable with asking questions of community members. Such intelligence gathering efforts can be critical to successful problem resolution.

Knowledge

A police officer should never assume that the individual with whom he is communicating is familiar with police procedures and understands what is expected of him. Such a lack of understanding is one reason for the reading of Miranda rights. While best practices in vehicle stops suggest that officer safety is increased by approaching in the subject's blind spots or under cover of blinding light, in practice this may mean that some subjects are confused and unsure of the situation and in turn are made more unpredictable and dangerous. It cannot be assumed that any individual already knows and fully comprehends the procedure for vehicle stops or any other type of police interaction. This is especially true in as heterogeneous a population as is found in Los Angeles. It is prudent to always seek to dispel uncertainty. Doing so may require officers to approach different situations differently depending on those with whom they are communicating, the situation in which the interaction is taking place, and other factors. Officers should seek to unambiguously communicate their intentions and how they expect those with whom they are communicating to respond to prevent the suspect, a bystander, or viewer on the evening news from misinterpreting the situation.

Experiences

It is a common observation in social psychology that a few vivid experiences can disproportionately color our perceptions of the world, often with one powerful, negative experience eclipsing many lesser positive experiences. Police officers cannot ensure that every interaction with the public is positive. What they can do is recognize that a given individual may have previous experiences that significantly influence his perception of the current situation. What does this mean in practice? An officer might, with a couple of respectful questions, learn information that critically figures in the outcome of the communication. As a notional example, on pulling a vehicle over he might ask, "Have you ever been stopped for a moving violation in California before?" This might seem simplistic, but it is an example of an easy way of establishing what the individual does or does not know. The response might well reveal much about the subject's state of mind and thus how he is likely to react to the events that follow.

Race

Much has been written on the issue of race and law enforcement issues. A simple point that bears highlighting is this: Equitable treatment under the law may well entail acknowledging and respecting racial differences rather than pretending they do not exist. For example, a white male police officer stopping a black male motorist in Los Angeles would be foolhardy not to at least inwardly prepare himself for the possibility that historical race relations in Los Angeles might influence the pending interaction. How might he approach the situation given this understanding? He should be prepared for the issue of race to be brought up overtly. He should consider approaching the situation in a manner that avoids invoking historical comparisons and otherwise steer the interaction away from potentially volatile ground.

Gender

As is the case with race, treating individuals equitably does not mean treating them as if they are genderless. Our society has well-developed discourses on male and female attitudes and behaviors that should be known by law enforcement personnel.

Occupation

Different jobs yield different skills, incomes, and lifestyles. Like other demographic factors, these differences figure prominently in an individual's perceptions and attitudes.

Residence

An individual encountered by the police officer may be local or visiting, may be a new transplant or a long-time resident of the area. He may be familiar or unfamiliar with local customs and history. A tourist from another country, for example, might act in a manner appropriate to his home country but not in keeping with police procedures in Los Angeles, and he might not understand the instructions given to him to correct his seemingly unresponsive behavior.

Arousal

This category can include an individual being fatigued, confused, hungry, having a rush of adrenalin, or in one of many other physiological or psychological states. The state of arousal significantly affects perceptions and cognition. Arousal can be generally seen as a negative influence when it comes to gaining voluntary compliance. Knowing that an individual may have adrenaline racing through his system or be panicked should prompt an officer to adapt his communication techniques. Adopting slower, simpler language and an even tone can prompt calming in some cases. Training should thoroughly address likely situations involving subjects in various states of agitation or arousal and provide officers with guidance on how to handle such cases.

Health

It should come as no surprise that health status can greatly influence an individual's cognitive processes. Physical illness can slow response times, distort sensory input, and otherwise interfere with the communication process. Mental illness is even more of a challenge to successful communication. For example, the individual who is in the grips of full-blown schizophrenia represents an exceedingly difficult subject from whom to gain voluntary compliance. He may not have the capability to understand the request, relate it to a course of action, or possess the faculties to act upon that course of action even if he wished to do so. Mental health workers have well-developed procedures for communicating with individuals suffering from a variety of mental illnesses; choosing the right one is often critical to the outcome of any such interaction. Police officers are likely to encounter at least as broad a range of mental illnesses in the course of their duties as many mental health workers. The difference is that police officers are too rarely trained in how to handle the range of such encounters, but they should be.

Affect

Affect is emotion. This category includes anger, fear, and other emotional states that color one's perceptions and actions. While often closely associated with arousal, the two are in fact distinct. Arousal is a measure of the physiological state of an individual, from quiet and peaceful to alert and charged with adrenaline. Affect is in contrast the emotional state of an individual. An officer should assess both a subject's state of arousal (discussed previously) *and* his affect. For example, a police officer encountering an individual in the midst of a spousal argument might find it counterproductive to assert a command presence. In some instances, assuming the role of mediator or peacemaker could be both more effective and a better course of action from the perspective of officer safety.

CATEGORY 3: ENVIRONMENT

Preparation Time

Generally, the more time and effort spent preparing a message, the more likely it is to be well crafted and complete. Having scripted dialogue pieces prepared and designed for particular circumstances can be very effective, although no script will handle all challenges. Well-honed tactical communication techniques, designed for a variety of circumstances and prepared in advance, are likely to improve officer interactions in general.

Duration of Exposure

Generally speaking, the longer a subject is exposed to a tactical communication—including its being repeated—the likelier that a subject will hear it and comprehend it in its entirety. This is purely a matter of transmitting the message accurately and completely. It may not influence whether it will be processed favorably by the listener.

Processing Time

Studies on resisting persuasion have shown that the longer a subject has to think about a persuasion attempt, the more comprehensive his thinking will be. Time may cause the subject to realize that compliance is in his best interests. Alternatively, if he can muster reasons and arguments against complying, he will be better able to access those options if given time. Conversely, shortening the time available reduces his ability to access counterarguments. For police officers, time granted an individual to think about the officer's orders, requests, or inquiries is a variable that should be controlled in accordance with what the officer wishes to accomplish. If the officer does not wish to give the individual the opportunity to argue, then he should speed the interaction accordingly. This might be perceived as coercive by subjects, however; and officers may sometimes want to extend the time available for subjects to think through the situation in order to (1) see the wisdom in complying and (2) feel that their compliance is not coerced.

Distraction

The more overwhelmed a subject is, the harder it is for him to think clearly. This load can be increased via ambient traffic noise, shouts and screams, multiple moving objects, bright lights, and many other factors. When possible, the level of distraction should be controlled by the officer. When impossible, the officer should factor into his own decisionmaking the likely effects that distractions might have on an individual's (and his own) decisionmaking.

Competition

When something actively interferes with the officer's communication, it unsurprisingly leads to greater difficulty in gaining voluntary compliance. Such interference might take the form of a bystander, crowd, or something the suspect recently saw on TV. Note that this can include accidental competition such as an officer speaking reassuringly but holding his weapon.

CATEGORY 4: THE FORMAT OF THE MESSAGE

Scale

It is important that any attempt at communication be appropriate to the subject audience in number and scope. A police officer can find himself speaking to an individual, a small group, or an enormous throng; the exact message should be different depending on the circumstances. The message should single individuals out to prevent diffusion of responsibility in some instances. A message should be inclusive if broad appeal is sought, aiming for common denominators among audience members. An officer should also choose how to frame a message appropriately. A message should seek voluntary compliance as part of an established pattern of abiding by laws for individuals with a history of legal compliance. Threats of coercion or identification of benefits to be gained in complying might be more effective approaches when addressing those with a history of non-compliance.

Medium

The medium of the message is the instrument used to deliver the persuasive communication: It could be the officer's voice, his gun, an official document, a badge, a loudspeaker, or any other physical channel used to transmit a message. Some media will directly pass the message to the subject, while others will act indirectly. Some media are verbal, and others are nonverbal. The choice of how to communicate with an audience is a vital one. What medium will be most effective? Some audiences do not mind being addressed over a public-address system, while others find it patronizing, unduly authoritative, or even hostile. An officer who wishes to communicate with any member of the public—bystander, suspect, attorney, or journalist, for example—should carefully consider which channel of communication is likely to be most effective, least ambiguous, and less likely to precipitate unintended consequences. This decision will be based on a range of variables involving a subject's perceptions. Pertinent questions for a police officer might include: Who is the subject audience? Who is nearby and likely to overhear or witness the interaction? What is going on in the vicinity? What are the trade-offs in officer safety in selecting one system in lieu of another?

ANALYSIS OF TRAINING COURSES

Table L.1 lists the variables that were used to assess each of the courses listed in Table L.2. Each variable was scored a "–" for "needs improvement," a "0" for "marginal," and a "+" for "good." In Table L.2, each course was given an overall rating with this same scoring key. For most of the courses, a combination of classroom observation, content analysis, and literature review were used to score the overall ratings and the assessment variables. Note that more than one of any letter (A–X) are listed for sorting purposes to highlight a + for one aspect and a – for another.

Table L.1

Assessment Variables

A.	Class objectives
B.	Instructional style
C.	Interactive learning setting
D.	Written curriculum quality
E.	Individual accountability
F.	Performance expectations
G.	Clear department values/context/policies/mandates
H.	Current topic-specific issues
I.	Adequacy of resources
J.	Professional ethical context setting
K.	Community policing/diversity context setting
L.	Tactical context setting
M.	Legal context
N.	Decisionmaking models
X.	Miscellaneous

Table L.2

Ratings and Comments on Training Courses

Course	Overall Rating		Comments
Use of Force—Recruit	–	A.	(–) Objectives as stated in curriculum not communicated through class instruction.
Use of Force, LD#20		B.	(–) Diversion from written curriculum.
Use of Force, Officer Survival		C.	(–) No participation solicited by instructor. Lecture format.
Use of Deadly Force—Impact weapon/exercise test		D.	(+) Comprehensive written curriculum.
		E.	(–) Ambiguity in consequences of actions.
		F.	(–) LAPD values unclear. Promotion criteria omitted.
		G.	(–) Lack of clarity of professional consequences for unethical actions.
		H.	(–) Lack of incorporation of field data into curriculum to enhance training on circumstances when force is employed.
		I.	(–) Apparent resource constraints. Quality of teaching aids is subpar.
		J.	(–) Underemphasis on importance of department ethics. Link between force and ethics is indistinct.
		K.	(–) No integration of community policing/diversity issues. Need to augment scenarios with current field data.
		N.	(+) Force continuum presented.

Table L.2—Continued

Course	Overall Rating	Comments
Use of Force—CED CEDP I CEDP II LETAC—Use of Force Policy LETAC—Use of Force "Table tops" LETAC—Deadly and Less Lethal Force options Supervisory Course Supervisor School—Use of Force Reporting Detective Supervisory Course	+	A. (+) Extensive presentation of factual information. Instructor adhered to class objectives. B. (+) Instructor set productive learning environment, facilitated discussion, promoted questioning, explored concerns. H. (+) Pertinent issues from the field/facts discussed. Consent decree acknowledged and described. L. (+) Tactical issues tied to context of use of force. M. (+) Background and history of policy presented. Importance to LAPD clearly iterated.
Search and Seizure—Recruit Search and Seizure LD#16 Vehicle Pullovers LD#22 Custody LD#31	0	D. (+) Curriculum is proficient in custody laws and citizen rights. H. (−) "Lessons Learned" data incorporation necessary for understanding of when search and seizure procedures are ineffective. K. (+) Steps to integrate "high risk" substance abusers, diversity issues, gender issues in curriculum. M. (−) Importance of legal search and seizure requires further discussion and linkage of issue back to rights of citizens.
Search and Seizure—CED Roll Call, Search and Seizure Detective Supervisory Course—Search Warrant CEDP I	0	D. (+) Clearly iterated definitions of relevant terms. K. (−) Curriculum lacks consideration of ethics and diversity issues. M. (+) Comprehensive content of legal information.

Table L.2—Continued

Course	Overall Rating	Comments
Arrest Procedures—Recruit Laws of Arrest LD#15 Juvenile Law and Procedure LD#11 Patrol Techniques LD#21 Handling Disputes LD#24 Arrest and Control Techniques LD#31 Crisis Intervention/Victim Assistance LD#4	0	D. (+) Curriculum is proficient on tactical arrest procedures. H. (–) Lessons learned needed to augment instruction. Identify what has been problematic with officer arrests. I. (–) Contextualization and anchoring of information needed to develop full understanding of practical applications of laws. K. (–) Integration of community policing/diversity issues needed. M. (+) Concise presentation of Constitutional Rights and importance of topic.
Arrest Procedures—CED Supervisory Development School—Criminal Law Update Watch Commander School—Law Update Arrest and Control Re-Certification Course CEDP—Firearms and Tactics CEDP 1	0	K. (–) Need more complete diversity discussion, ethics, and community policing information. Course serves as refresher and update on new law—meets this end, but fails to tie new laws and procedures back to community policing. L. (+) The topics covered are physical tactics. Fragmented into very specific areas (e.g., bus stops). M. (+) Laws of arrest clearly presented in curriculum.

Table L.2—Continued

Course	Overall Rating	Comments
Community Policing—Recruit Community Policing/Problem Solving LD#3 Tactical Communication LD#3	0	K. (+) Cultural differences within the neighborhood discussed. K. (−) Minimal contextualization. (Based on observation only—LD does not appear to be applicable to the topic.) N. (+) Clear presentation of community policing/problem-solving model. P. (+) Clear definition of community policing. The role of a community policing officer clearly defined.
Community Policing—CED Supervisor Course COP/POP (community-oriented policing/problem-oriented policing)	0	A. (+) Course objectives outlined in the lesson plan congruent with classroom presentation, although a number of topics were skipped or covered briefly. E. (+) The role of a community policing officer clearly defined. K. (+) Rationale for community policing provided. K. (−) Community expectations not explicitly stated. Minimal contextualization. N. (−) No presentation of community policing/problem-solving models (e.g., SARA). P. (+) Clear iteration of community policing. The role of a community policing officer clearly defined.

Table L.2—Continued

Course	Overall Rating	Comments
Diversity—Recruit Persons with Disabilities/Special Needs LD#37 Cultural Diversity LD#42	+	D. (+) Debriefing is adequate throughout the lessons. E. (+) Personal biases discussed. K. (+) Partial discussion on applicability to real-life experiences. Sexual orientation (within and outside of the agency considered). Specific issues relevant to persons with disabilities and mental illnesses presented. Issues relevant to racial/ethnic minorities discussed, generally. K. (−) Issues relevant to racial/ethnic minorities discussed, generally. Community variations and expectations not presented. (This is all based on the content analysis, not on the observations.) P. (+) Clear definitions of important concepts (e.g., prejudice, stereotypes, and discrimination).
Diversity—CED Tools for Tolerance	−	No formal diversity awareness class at the CE level. There is a diversity and discrimination in the workplace class offered that concentrates mostly on diversity and discrimination inside the Department.

Table L.2—Continued

Course	Overall Rating		Comments
Values, Ethics, Supervision[a]	+		
History Professionalism and Ethics LD#1		A.	(+) Meets course objectives.
		A.	(−) Supervision course could benefit from fully developed course outline/objectives stated up front.
Ethical Dimensions of Leadership		B.	(+) Interactive discussions with lively debate and active participation.
Supervision/Watch Commander		C.	(+) Interactive discussions with lively debate and active participation.
		D.	(+) Good use of assessment tools in ethics seminar.
		D.	(−) Supervision course lacking materials.
		E.	(+) Emphasis on personal accountability and leadership values.
		F.	(+) Importance of going into the field stressed. Outlined the need for feedback from above and below.
		G.	(+) Specific reference made to LAPD values and mission. Specific reference and acknowledgment of demands of consent decree. Stressed explaining historical context of policies to subordinates.
		J.	(+) Appeal to broader organizational goals and concept of professional standards and ethics—idea of being an advocate for the LAPD. Discussion of hallmarks of positive leadership.
		X.	(+) High-level commanders/captains very engaged in ethics discussions.

Table L.2—Continued

Course	Overall Rating	Comments
Field Training Officer	–	A. (–) Needs more complete course outline/objectives stated up front. Objectives were not fully met.
		B. (–) Several disconnects between what was being taught and how instructor worked with class (e.g., adult learning principles were described, but not fully applied). Reliance on lecture-based model here in opposition to use of adult learning principles and problem-based learning techniques.
		D. (+) Components of the written materials are strong, though they are not fully delivered (e.g., facilitation skills workbook).
		H. (–) FTO program is not best practice in field, should reassess in light of Reno's and other departments' problem-oriented models.
		J. (–) Insufficient context setting for FTOs as department role models.
		N. (–) Inadequate discussion of the methods for evaluation of probationers.
		X. FTO training is philosophically inconsistent with teaching in recruit academy.

Table L.2—Continued

Course	Overall Rating		Comments
Instructor Development	0	A.	(−) Several disconnects between what was being taught and how instructor worked with class.
		B.	(+) Use of many instructional techniques in class, modeling of techniques for students. Learning activities, such as the training-needs analysis, are effective.
		B.	(−) Several disconnects between what was being taught and how instructor worked with class (e.g., adult learning principles were described, but not fully applied). Reliance on lecture-based model in opposition to use of adult learning principles and problem-based learning techniques.
		C.	(+) Learning activities, such as the training needs analysis, are effective.
		D.	(+) Written materials strong and thorough but not fully utilized; given as handouts but time is not spent to familiarize students or to contextualize materials.
		D.	(−) One major omission in written materials is failure to mention scenario or problem-based learning. Course curriculum not at the level of best practice in industry and could be improved through use of external expertise.
		L.	(−) Written materials strong and thorough but not fully utilized; given as handouts but time is not spent to familiarize students or to contextualize materials. Learning activities, such as the training-needs analysis, are effective but not fully debriefed/contextualized in class.
		X.	(−) Unsystematic implementation—this training of trainers is not delivered consistently for all trainers.

Table L.2—Continued

Course	Overall Rating	Comments
CEDP	+	
CEDP I		A. (+) Objectives were clear in written materials and adhered to in course.
CEDP V		B. (+ and –) Instructors were versed in and used many instructional techniques. Instructors needed more time working together (made conflicting statements), and needed more time on debriefing.
		C. (+) Many interactive teaching techniques were employed to keep the class interested and involved.
		D. (+) Thorough materials.
		F. (+) Expectations of officers were made clear, with attention paid to different circumstances.
		H. (+) Broad context of topic, including current law and policy, was covered.
		H. (–) Instructors differed over policies and gave different opinions on individual and managerial accountability.
		K. (–) This area was not well identified or described.
		L. (+) Tactical maneuvers were thoroughly debriefed.
		M. (+) The legal context was presented for different situations.

[a]Content analysis conducted for "Leadership in the 21st Century" ethics seminar only.

NOTES: Not all of the analysis methods apply to each course. The analysis categories were as follows: A. Class objectives, B. Instructional style, C. Interactive learning setting, D. Written curriculum quality, E. Individual accountability, F. Performance expectations, G. Clear department values/context/policies/mandates, H. Current topic-specific issues, I. Adequacy of resources, J. Professional ethical context setting, K. Community policing/diversity context setting, L. Tactical context setting, M. Legal context, N. Decision-making models, X. Miscellaneous.

SUMMARY OF RECOMMENDATIONS

OVERARCHING RECOMMENDATION

The Los Angeles Police Department should adopt a concept of police professionalism that incorporates the tenets of corporateness, responsibility, and expertise as the mechanism for guiding the development and execution of its training, which will include training in the areas of use of force, search and seizure, arrest procedures, community policing, and diversity awareness.

PRIMARY RECOMMENDATIONS

Establish an LAPD Lessons-Learned Program

- Assign the training group primary responsibility for the lessons-learned program.

- Establish and maintain lessons-learned links with other police departments and law enforcement agencies.

- Encourage but do not pressure contributors to provide contact information. Remember that the receipt of quality lessons learned is the primary goal.

- Establish an LAPD lessons-learned web page that promotes submissions from the field and community.

- Create standing distribution lists to facilitate timely and efficient distribution of lessons-learned products.

Introduce and Maintain Consistently High Quality Throughout Every Aspect of LAPD Training

- Clearly articulate the type of officer the Department wants to develop, and use police training to model the behaviors expected of police personnel.

- Employ theoretically grounded adult educational techniques such as interactive methods and self-directed learning.

- Maintain consistent and high-quality curriculum design and instructor performance throughout the Department.

- Develop uniform format guidelines for written curriculum materials and revise instructional materials to meet those guidelines. Complete Department-wide revisions no later than March 31, 2006.

- Vest the training group with the power to validate instructors before they are allowed to train others and to remove instructors who fail to maintain acceptable levels of training performance.

- Do not allow any LAPD instructor to train officers prior to his successful completion of the Department instructor development course.

- Teach LAPD instructors via the same curricular format and organization that they will be expected to teach.

- Implement procedures to use all four levels of the Kirkpatrick model to evaluate Department training effectiveness.

Restructure the LAPD Training Group to Allow the Centralization of Planning; Instructor Qualification, Evaluation, and Learning Retention; and More Efficient Use of Resources

- Carefully plan and implement restructuring to minimize organizational and personal turbulence.

- Carefully coordinate reorganization with any further automation of training group functions.

- Introduce an automated learning management system as discussed in Appendix I.

- Conduct an intra-Department analysis of training coordinator usage to determine how many positions should be assigned to the training group and how many others can be consolidated.

- Conduct further analyses of instructor positions, both before and after consolidation, to determine where additional redundancies exist.

Integrate Elements of Community-Oriented Policing and Diversity Awareness Training Models Throughout LAPD Training

- Make the LAPD a more "transparent agency," open to the entire community.

- Develop and articulate a clear and unified message regarding community policing.

- Actively recruit diverse individuals who possess the appropriate values and skills necessary for community policing within diverse communities.

- Train all LAPD personnel in the community-policing problem-solving model.

- Consider adopting the CAPRA problem-solving model in lieu of the SARA approach.

- Maintain, refine, and augment the LAPD's ongoing community engagement activities, including the citizen police academy.

  — Provide more training on community policing, problem solving, and diversity awareness.

  — Thoroughly integrate community policing, problem solving, and diversity awareness into training (rather than teaching them in separate, stand-alone blocks as has been suggested in previous studies).

  — Carefully craft classroom scenarios and case studies to reflect real-life community dynamics that officers are likely to encounter (i.e., diverse groups of people with a variety of problems).

— Better emphasize a problem-solving approach and application of problem-solving skills in classroom scenarios and case studies.

— Include community policing activities for recruit field training.

— Increase training involving participation by community members.

• Increase the length of the community policing course and use it for induction purposes.

• Adopt as permanent the ongoing trial of introducing the basics of community policing and diversity awareness early in academy training and integrate community policing, problem solving, and diversity awareness throughout pertinent recruit instruction. Broaden this effort through field training and continuing education.

• Involve recruits in problem-solving projects and encourage recruits to participate in various community activities during the training period.

• Develop problem-based scenarios and case studies that allow recruits to apply problem-solving skills and knowledge of diverse populations.

• Base the training approach on the tenets of adult education, promoting decisionmaking ability and initiative within the community.

• Involve recruits in area SLO summit meetings and use qualified SLOs for academy training.

• Discuss existing community problems in class in addition to problem-based scenarios and case studies.

• Use SLOs as facilitators for training and consider increasing the use of civilian instructors and guest speakers from the community in training.

Develop Training on Use of Force, Search and Seizure, and Arrest Procedures That Meets Current Standards of Excellence

- Use contextualization to enhance realism in training and enrich learning processes.

- Use contextualized learning techniques to integrate topic areas in training curriculum.

- Use lessons learned to create realistic scenarios for classroom training.

- Complement recruit learning domains with *specific* communication techniques for diverse and special-needs populations.

- Develop training on tactical communication in proportion to the frequency that it is used in the field.

Adams, K., et al., *Use of Force by Police: Overview of National and Local Data*, Washington, D.C.: U.S. Department of Justice, National Institute of Justice and Bureau of Justice Statistics, NCJ 176330, October 1999.

Albrecht, Steven, and John Morrison, *Contact & Cover: Two-Officer Suspect Control*, Springfield, Ill.: Charles C. Thomas, 1992.

Alliger, George M., and Elizabeth A. Janak, "Kirkpatrick's Levels of Training Criteria: Thirty Years Later," *Personnel Psychology*, Vol. 42, 1989.

Alpert, Geoffrey P., and Roger G. Dunham, *Policing Multi-Ethnic Neighborhoods: The Miami Study and Findings for Law Enforcement in the United States*, New York: Greenwood Press, 1988.

Alpert, Geoffrey P., et al., eds., *Community Policing: Contemporary Readings*, 2nd ed., Prospect Heights, Ill.: Waveland Press, 2000.

Aronson, E., *The Social Animal*, 7th ed., New York: W. H. Freeman, 1995.

Bettinghaus, Erwin P., "The Influence of the Communicator," in *Persuasive Communication*, 3rd ed., 1980a, pp. 89–108.

———, "Structuring Messages and Appeals," in *Persuasive Communication*, 3rd ed., 1980b, pp. 133–152.

Bratton, William J., and William Andrews, "What We've Learned About Policing," *City Journal*, 1999, pp. 14–27.

Caffarella, Rosemary S., *Planning Programs for Adult Learners: A Practical Guide for Educators, Trainers, and Staff Developers*, 2nd ed. [Higher and Adult Education Series], San Francisco, Calif.: Jossey-Bass, 2002.

California Department of Justice, Office of the Attorney General, Crime and Violence Prevention Center, *Community Oriented Policing and Problem Solving: Definitions and Principles*, Sacramento, February 1999. Available online at www.safestate.org/shop/files/DefsPrin.pdf, last accessed March 26, 2003.

Callahan, J., "Use of Force After the Rodney King Incident," *The Tactical Edge*, Fall 1992, pp. 17–19.

Carlson, Daniel P., *When Cultures Clash: The Divisive Nature of Police-Community Relations and Suggestions for Improvement*, Upper Saddle River, N.J.: Prentice Hall, 2002.

Carter, David L., *Human Resource Issues for Community Policing*, School of Criminal Justice, Michigan State University, www.cj.msu.edu/~people/cp/humres.html, accessed February 17, 2003.

Center for Army Lessons Learned, *History of the Army's Lessons Learned System*, http://call.army.mil/products/handbook/97-13/history.htm, accessed February 14, 2003.

Chaiken, S., "The Heuristic Model of Persuasion," in M. P. Zanna, J. M. Olson, and C. P. Herman, eds., *Social Influence: The Ontario Symposium*, Vol. 5, Hillsdale, N.J.: Lawrence Erlbaum Associates, Inc., 1987, pp. 3–39.

Christopher Commission report. See Independent Commission of the Los Angeles Police Department.

Cialdini, R. B., *Influence: Science and Practice*, 2nd ed., New York: Harper Collins, 1988.

Consent decree. See *United States of America v. City of Los Angeles*.

Dey, I., *Qualitative Data Analysis: A User-Friendly Guide for Social Scientists*, London: Routledge, 1993.

Dossey, Greg [The Civilian Martial Arts Advisory Panel], *Arrest and Control Instructor Manual*, Los Angeles Police Department, March 1997.

Eisenhardt, K. M., "Building Theories from Case Study Research," *Academy of Management Review*, October 1989, Vol. 14, No. 4, pp. 532–550.

Evers, T. E., J. C. Rush, and I. Berdrow, *The Bases of Competence: Skills for Lifelong Learning and Employability*, San Francisco, Calif.: Jossey-Bass, 1998.

Fagan, Patrick, *Effective Search and Seizure*, University of Mississippi, 1997. Available online at www.fsu.edu/~crimdo/fagan.html, last accessed July 16, 2002.

Fenstermacher, Gary D., and Jonas F. Soltis, *Approaches to Teaching*, 2nd ed., New York: Columbia University, Teachers College Press, 1992.

Ficarrottal, J. Carl, "Are Military Professionals Bound by a Higher Moral Standard?" *Armed Forces & Society*, Vol. 24, Fall 1997, pp. 59–75.

Fiske, S. T., and S. E. Taylor, *Social Cognition*, New York: McGraw-Hill, 1991.

Fyfe, J. J., et al., *Police Administration*, 5th ed., Boston: McGraw-Hill, 1997.

Garvin, D. A., "Building a Learning Organization," in *Harvard Business Review on Knowledge Management*, Cambridge, Mass.: Harvard Business School Press, 1998.

Gates, Daryl F., *A Training Analysis of the Los Angeles Police Department*, Los Angeles Police Department, October 21, 1991.

Geller, William A., and Hans Toch, eds., *Police Violence: Understanding and Controlling Police Abuse of Force*, New Haven, Conn.: Yale University Press, 1996.

Gillespie, T. T., D. G. Hart, and J. D. Boren, *Police Use of Force: A Line Officer's Guide*, Kansas City: Varro Press, 1998.

Glenn, Russell W., *Reading Athena's Dance Card: Men Against Fire in Vietnam*, Annapolis, Md.: Naval Institute Press, 2000.

Glickman, Carl D., Stephen P. Gordon, and Jovita J. Ross-Gordon, *Supervision of Instruction: A Developmental Approach*, 3rd edition, Needham Heights, Mass.: Allyn & Bacon, 1995.

Goldstein, Herman, *Problem-Oriented Policing*, Philadelphia: Temple University Press, 1990.

Greenfield, L. A., P. A. Langan, and S. K. Smith [Bureau of Justice Statistics], with R. J. Kaminski [National Institute of Justice], *Police Use of Force: Collection of National Data*, Washington, D.C.: U.S. Department of Justice [jointly published with the National Institute of Justice], NCJ-165040, November 1997. Available online at www.ojp.usdoj.gov/bjs/pub/pdf/puof.pdf, last accessed March 25, 2003.

Hall, H., "Six Steps to Developing a Successful E-Learning Initiative: Excerpts from the E-Learning Guidebook," in Allison Rossett, ed., *The ASTD E-Learning Handbook: Best Practices, Strategies, and Case Studies for an Emerging Field*, New York: McGraw-Hill, 2002.

Haney, Hutch, *Notes from Adult Development Course*, Seattle University, 1998.

Himelfarb, Frum, "A Training Strategy for Policing in a Multicultural Society," *The Police Chief*, November 1991.

"History of the Army's Lessons Learned System," in *A Guide to the Services and the Gateway of the Center for Army Lessons Learned*, Handbook No. 97-13, Fort Leavenworth, Kan.: U.S. Center for Army Lessons Learned, circa 1997. Available online at http://call.army.mil/products/handbook/97-13/history.htm, last accessed March 25, 2003.

Hoover, Jerry, Gerard Cleveland, and Greg Saville, "A New Generation of Field Training: The Reno PTO Model," in Melissa Reuland, Corina Sole Briot, and Lisa Carroll, eds., *Solving Crime and Disorder Problems: Current Issues, Police Strategies, and Organizational Tactics*, Washington, D.C.: Police Executive Research Forum, 2001, pp. 175–189.

Hovland, Carl I., Irving L. Janis, and Harold H. Kelly, "Credibility of the Communicator," in *Communication and Persuasion: Psychological Studies of Opinion Change*, New Haven, Conn.: Yale University Press, 1953, pp. 19–55.

Hovland, Carl I., Arthur A. Lumsdaine, and Fred D. Sheffield, "The Effect of Presenting 'One Side' Versus 'Both Sides' in Changing Opinions on a Controversial Subject," in Wilbur Schramm and Donald F. Roberts, eds., *The Process and Effects of Mass Communication*, 2nd ed., University of Illinois Press, 1974, pp. 3–53.

Hovland, Carl I., and Walter Weiss, "The Influence of Source Credibility on Communication Effectiveness," *Public Opinion Quarterly*, 1951, pp. 635–650.

Huntington, Samuel P., *The Soldier and the State: The Theory and Politics of Civil-Military Relations*, New York: Vintage, 1957.

Independent Commission of the Los Angeles Police Department, *Report*, July 9, 1991. (This document is commonly referred to as the Christopher Commission report.)

International Association of Chiefs of Police, *Police Use of Force in America*, Washington, D.C., 2001.

Iyengar, Shanto, and Donald R. Kinder, *News That Matters*, Chicago: University of Chicago Press, 1987.

Jarvis, Peter, John Holford, and Colin Griffin, *The Theory and Practice of Learning*, Sterling, Va.: Stylus Publishing Inc., 1998.

Jenkins, Patrick, "Happiness Sheets Are Just a Start: Monitoring Results," *Financial Times* [London], June 25, 2002.

Jones, Arthur A., and Robin Wiseman, *Bratton's Drumbeat: How Does the Chief Really Intend to Fight the Gang War?* www.lacp.org/Articles%20-%20Expert%20-%20Our%20Opinion/030112-Brattons Drumbeat-AJ.html, last accessed March 8, 2003.

Joyce, Bruce, and Marsha Weil, *Models of Teaching*, 5th ed., Needham Heights, Mass.: Allyn & Bacon, 1996.

Kahneman, D., and A. Tversky, "Choice, Values, and Frames," *American Psychologist*, Vol. 39, 1984, pp. 341–350.

————, "Prospect Theory: An Analysis of Decision Under Risk," *Econometrica*, Vol. 47, No. 2, March 1979, pp. 263–292.

————, "The Psychology of Preferences," *Scientific American*, Vol. 246, 1982, pp. 160–173.

Kaminsky, Glenn, *The Field Training Concept in Criminal Justice Agencies*, Upper Saddle River, N.J.: Prentice Hall, 2000.

Kelling, G. L., and C. M. Coles, *Fixing Broken Windows: Restoring Order and Reducing Crime in Our Communities*, New York: Simon & Schuster, 1996.

Kennedy, Rozella Floranz, ed., *Fighting Police Abuse: A Community Action Manual*, 2nd ed., New York: American Civil Liberties Union, ACLU Department of Public Education, 1997. Available online at www.aclu.org/PolicePractices/PolicePractices.cfm?ID= 5009&c=25&Type=s, last accessed March 25, 2003.

Kirkpatrick, Donald L., *Evaluating Training Programs*, San Francisco, Calif.: Berrett-Koehler, 1998.

Knowles, M. S., E. F. Holton III, and R. A. Swanson, *The Adult Learner: The Definitive Classic in Adult Education and Human Resource Development*, 5th ed., Woburn, Mass.: Butterworth-Heinemann, 1998.

Kusy, M. E., Jr., *The Effects of Types of Training Evaluation on Support of Training Among Corporation Managers* [Training and Development Research Center Project Number 12], St. Paul, Minn.: Minnesota University Department of Vocational and Technical Education, 1986.

Laird, Lorelei, "Bratton Pledges to Restore LAPD's 'Tarnished' Reputation as Police Chief," *Metropolitan News-Enterprise*, October 4, 2002, p. 8. Available online at www.metnews.com/articles/ brat100402.htm, last accessed March 25, 2003.

Leming, Robert S., *Teaching About the Fourth Amendment's Protection Against Unreasonable Searches and Seizures*, Bloomington, Ind.: ERIC Clearinghouse for Social Studies/Social Science Education, 1993. Available online at www.ed.gov/databases/

ERIC_Digests/ed363526.html [redirects to www.ericfacility.net/ericdigests/ed363526.html], last accessed March 25, 2003.

Los Angeles Board of Police Commissioners, *In the Course of Change: The Los Angeles Police Department Five Years After the Christopher Commission*, May 30, 1996.

Los Angeles Police Department, *Introduction to Case Study Training*, document supported by Grant #970CWX0006 awarded by the U.S. Department of Justice, Office of Community Oriented Policing Services (COPS), 2001.

Los Angeles Police Department, "Los Angeles Police Department Core Values," in *2000 Manual of the Los Angeles Police Department*, www.lapdonline.org/dept%5Fmanual/core%5Fvalues.htm, last accessed March 25, 2003a.

Los Angeles Police Department, "Mission Statement," in *Department Motto, Mission Statement, Values and Principles*, www.lapdonline.org/general_information/dept_mission_statement/mission_stmnt.htm, last accessed March 25, 2003b.

Los Angeles Police Department, "Management Principles," in *Department Motto, Mission Statement, Values and Principles*, www.lapdonline.org/general_information/dept_mission_statement/mgmnt_principles.htm, accessed February 7, 2003c.

Los Angeles Police Department, *Community Police Academy for Young Adults*, http://216.41.186.4/community/ocb/ocb_police_academy.htm, accessed on March 8, 2003d.

Los Angeles Police Department, "Core Values," in *Department Motto, Mission Statement, Values and Principles*, www.lapdonline.org/general_information/dept_mission_statement/core_values.htm, last accessed March 25, 2003e.

Los Angeles Police Department, "To Protect and To Serve," in *Department Motto, Mission Statement Values and Principles*, www.lapdonline.org/general%5Finformation/dept%5Fmission%5Fstatement/dept%5Fmission%5Fmain.htm, last accessed March 25, 2003f.

Los Angeles Police Department Manual, www.lapd.org/dept%5Fmanual/core%5Fvalues.htm, accessed February 10, 2003.

Los Angeles Police Department web site, www.lapd.org, accessed March 11, 2003.

Los Angeles Police Department, Management Services Division, *Department Analysis of Rampart Independent Review Panel Recommendations,* January 25, 2001.

Los Angeles Police Department, Training Division, "Custody," in *Los Angeles Police Department Recruit Training Program,* LD #31, prepared by the Academics Instruction Training Unit, revised 2001a.

Los Angeles Police Department, Training Division, "Laws of Arrest," in *Los Angeles Police Department Recruit Training Program,* LD #15, prepared by Academics Instruction Training Unit, revised 2001b, p. 17.

Los Angeles Police Department, Training Division, "Search and Seizure," in *Los Angeles Police Department Recruit Training Program,* LD #16, prepared by Academics Instruction Training Unit, revised 2001c.

Maheswaran, D., and J. Meyers-Levy, "The Influence of Message Framing and Issue Involvement," *Journal of Marketing Research,* Vol. 27, 1990, pp. 361–367.

Mastrofski, Stephen D., "What Does Community Policing Mean for Daily Police Work?" *National Institute of Justice Journal,* Vol. 225, August 1992, pp. 23–27.

Mathieu, J. E., S. I. Tannenbaum, and E. Salas, "Influences of Individual and Situational Characteristics on Measures of Training Effectiveness," *The Academy of Management Journal,* Vol. 35, No. 4, October 1992, pp. 828–847.

Matthews, Lloyd J., "Is the Military Profession Legitimate?" *Army,* January 1994, pp. 15–23.

McLaughlin, Vance, *Police and the Use of Force: The Savannah Study,* Westport, Conn.: Praeger, 1992.

McShane, Larry, *Cops Under Fire: The Reign of Terror Against Hero Cops*, Washington, D.C.: Regnery Publishing, 1999.

Michigan State Police, Training Division, *Michigan State Police, Staff Orientation Manual*, Lansing, 2001.

Millett, Allan R., *Military Professionalism and Officership in America*, Mershon Center, Briefing Paper Number Two, Columbus, Ohio: The Ohio State University, 1977.

Milton, Catherine H., et al., eds., *Police Use of Deadly Force*, Washington, D.C.: Police Foundation, 1977.

Moran, J. V., "Top Ten E-Learning Myths," in Allison Rossett, ed., *The ASTD E-Learning Handbook: Best Practices, Strategies, and Case Studies for an Emerging Field*, New York: McGraw-Hill, 2002.

Murphy, William, and George Gascón, *Continuing Education Development Plan*, LAPD, June 2001.

Nadler, Leonard, and Zeace Nadler, *Designing Training Programs: The Critical Events Model*, Houston: Gulf Publishing, 1994.

NOLO Law for All, *Understanding Search and Seizure Law*, Berkeley, Calif., www.nolo.com/lawcenter/ency/article.cfm/objectID/DED 24689-ADA8-4785-887A0B4A19A694DE, accessed July 16, 2002.

Parks, Bernard, "The State of Community Policing: On the New Los Angeles Police Department," *Management Paper*, Vol. 1, October 1997, p. 1.

Peak, Kenneth J., and Ronald W. Glensor, *Community Policing and Problem Solving: Strategies and Practices*, Upper Saddle River, N.J.: Prentice Hall, 1996.

———, *Policing America: Methods, Issues, Challenges*, Englewood Cliffs, N.J.: Regents/Prentice Hall, 1993.

Pedicelli, Gabriella, *When Police Kill: Police Use of Force in Montréal and Toronto*, Montréal: Véhicule Press, 1998.

Penn State College of Education, "Principles of the Framework," in *Foundation Skills—Framework for Building Pennsylvania's Work-*

force, www.ed.psu.edu/foundationskills/Introduction/4principles. asp, last accessed March 26, 2003.

Petty, Richard E., and J. T. Cacioppo, "Central and Peripheral Routes of Persuasion: Application to Advertising," in L. Percy and Arch G. Woodside, eds., *Advertising and Consumer Psychology*, Lexington, Mass.: Lexington Books, 1983, pp. 3–23.

Petty, R. E., and J. T. Cacioppo, *Communication and Persuasion: Central and Peripheral Routes to Attitude Change*, New York: Springer-Verlag, 1986.

Petty, R. E., J. T. Cacioppo, and R. Cialdini, "Attitude and Attitude Change," in M. Rosenzweis and L. Porter, eds., *Annual Review of Psychology*, Vol. 32, 1981.

Petty, R. E., T. M. Ostrom, and T. C. Brock, *Cognitive Responses in Persuasion*, Hillsdale, N.J.: Lawrence Erlbaum Associates, Inc., 1981.

Piskurich, G. M., *Rapid Instructional Design: Learning ID Fast and Right*, San Francisco, Calif.: Jossey-Bass, 2000.

Pratkanis, A., and E. Aronson, *Age of Propaganda*, New York: Freedman, 1992.

"Predicting the Retention of Proficiency at 16 Common Tasks," *ARI Newsletter*, Vol. 12, No. 2, undated, pp. 10–12. Available online at www.ari.army.mil, last accessed June 20, 2003.

Putnam, L. L., and M. Holmer, "Framing, Reframing, and Issue Development: Communication and Negotiation," in Linda L. Putman and Michael E. Roloff, eds., *Sage Annual Reviews of Communication Research*, Newbury Park, Calif.: Sage Publications, Inc., Vol. 20., 1992, pp. 128–155.

Rampart Independent Review Panel, *Report of the Rampart Independent Review Panel*, Los Angeles, November 2000.

Rippa, S. Alexander, ed., *Educational Ideas in America: A Documentary History*, New York: David McKay Company, 1969.

Roney, C. J. R., E. T. Higgins, and J. Shah, "Goals and Framing: How Outcome Focus Influences Motivation and Emotion," *Personality and Social Psychology Bulletin*, Vol. 21, No. 11, 1995, pp. 1151–1160.

Rosemann, M., "Teaching Enterprise Systems in a Distance Education Mode," in R. Discernza, C. Howard, and K. Schenk, eds., *The Design & Management of Effective Distance Learning Programs*, Hershey, Pa.: Idea Group, 2002.

Rossett, Allison, ed., *The ASTD E-Learning Handbook: Best Practices, Strategies, and Case Studies for an Emerging Field*, New York: McGraw-Hill, 2002.

Salopek, Jennifer J., "Training Design and Delivery," *Training & Development*, Vol. 53, No. 5, May 1999.

Schank, R. C., *Designing World Class E-Learning: How IBM, GE, Harvard Business School and Columbia University Are Succeeding at E-Learning*, New York: McGraw-Hill, 2002.

Scott, Michael S., *Problem Oriented Policing: Reflections on the First 20 Years*, Washington, D.C.: U.S. Department of Justice, Office of Community Oriented Policing Services, 2000.

Seattle Police Department, *Beyond the Badge: Discrimination vs. Discretion*, video, April 2001a.

Seattle Police Department, *Racial Discrimination vs. Discretion*, video, WSCJTC, April 4, 2001b.

Seattle Police Department, *Training of Trainers*, 1996.

Shafir, E., I. Simonson, and A. Tversky, "Reason-based Choice," *Cognition*, Vol. 49, 1993, pp. 11–36.

Shusta, Robert M., Deena R. Levine, Philip R. Harris, and Herbert Z. Wong, *Multicultural Law Enforcement: Strategies for Peacekeeping in a Diverse Society*, Englewood Cliffs, N.J.: Prentice-Hall, 1995.

Simonson, I., and A. Tversky, "Choice in Context: Tradeoff Contrast and Extremeness Aversion," *Journal of Marketing Research*, Vol. 29, 1992, pp. 281–295.

Skolnick, J. H., and J. J. Fyfe, *Above the Law: Police and the Excessive Use of Force*, New York: The Free Press, 1993.

Sloan, R., R. C. Trojanowicz, and B. Buqueroux, *Basic Issues in Training: A Foundation for Community Policing—Making the Transition to Mission Driven Training*, Lansing, Mich.: National Center for Community Policing, Michigan State University, www.cj.msu.edu/~people/cp/basic.html, last accessed May 29, 2003.

Smith, S. M., and R. E. Petty, "Message Framing and Persuasion: A Message Processing Analysis," *Personality and Social Psychology Bulletin*, Vol. 22, No. 3, 1996, pp. 257–268.

Smith, S. M., and D. R. Shaffer, "Celerity and Cajolery: Rapid Speech May Promote or Inhibit Persuasion Through Its Impact on Message Elaboration," *Personality and Social Psychology Bulletin*, Vol. 17, 1991, pp. 663–669.

Snyder, M., E. D. Tanke, and E. Berscheid, "Social Perception and Interpersonal Behavior: On the Self-Fulfilling Nature of Social Stereotypes," *Journal of Personality and Social Psychology*, Vol. 35, 1977, pp. 656–666.

Stevens, Dennis J., *Case Studies in Community Policing*, Upper Saddle River, N.J.: Prentice Hall, 2001.

Strauss, A., and J. Corbin, *Basics of Qualitative Research*, Newbury Park, Calif.: SAGE Publications, 1990.

Tamm, Quinn, editorial, in Nelson A. Wilson, ed., *Police and the Changing Community: Selected Reading*, Washington, D.C.: International Association of Chiefs of Police, 1965.

Tita, G., K. J. Riley, and P. W. Greenwood, "From Boston to Boyle Heights: The Process and Prospects of a 'Pulling Levers' Strategy in a Los Angeles Barrio," in S. Decker, ed., *Gangs, Youth Violence and Community Policing*, Belmont: Wadsworth Press, forthcoming.

Tiwana, A., *The Knowledge Management Toolkit: Practical Techniques for Building a Knowledge Management System*, Upper Saddle River, N.J.: Prentice Hall, 1999.

United States of America v. City of Los Angeles, California, Board of Police Commissioners of the City of Los Angeles, and the Los Angeles

Police Department Consent Decree of June 15, 2001. (Also called the consent decree.)

U.S. Census Bureau, *Census of Population and Housing: Summary File 1*, 2000.

U.S. Census Bureau, *State and County QuickFacts*, http://quickfacts. census.gov/qfd/, last accessed May 30, 2003.

U.S. Constitution, online version prepared by Gerald Murphy (Cleveland Free-Net—aa300) [distributed by the Cybercasting Services Division of the National Public Telecomputing Network (NPTN)], http://lcweb2.loc.gov/const/const.html, last accessed March 25, 2003.

U.S. Department of Justice, U.S. Office of Justice Programs, Bureau of Justice Assistance [prepared by the Community Policing Consortium], *Understanding Community Policing: A Framework for Action*, Washington, D.C.: U.S. Government Printing Office, NCJ-148457, August 1994. Available online at www.ncjrs.org/pdffiles/commp.pdf, last accessed March 26, 2003.

Visitor Information: The Memorial Amphitheater at Arlington National Cemetery, www.arlingtoncemetery.org/visitor_information/amphitheater.html, accessed February 7, 2003.

Walker, Decker F., and Jonas F. Soltis, *Curriculum and Aims*, 2nd ed., New York: Columbia University, Teachers College Press, 1992.

Walker, S., C. Archbold, and L. Herbst, *Mediating Citizen Complaints Against Police Officers: A Guide for Police and Community Leaders*, Washington, D.C.: U.S. Department of Justice, Office of Community Oriented Policing Service, Grant 1999-CK-WX-1016, 2002.

Weisburd, D., R. Greenspan, E. E. Hamilton, H. Williams, and K. A. Bryant, "Police Attitudes Toward Abuse of Authority: Findings From a National Study," *Research in Brief*, Washington, D.C.: U.S. Department of Justice, National Institute of Justice, NCJ 181312, May 2000.

Welsh, Robert F., and Lucille M. Bell, *React, Fire, Win: Defensive Police Tactics*, Westerville, Ohio: WINCOM, 1983.

Williams, G. T.,"Force Continuums: A Liability to Law Enforcement?" *FBI Law Enforcement Bulletin*, June 2002, pp. 14–19.

Wilson, J. Q., and G. L. Kelling, "Broken Windows: The Police and Neighborhood Safety," *The Atlantic Monthly,* March 1982, pp. 29–38.

Zuboff, S., *In the Age of the Smart Machine: The Future of Work and Power,* New York: Basic Books, 1988.